P9-DCV-788

Christian
Mythology

3 95

Christian Mythology

George Every

Hamlyn

Colour Plates

For my god-daughter,
Katherine Davison

The Hamlyn Publishing Group Limited
London New York Sydney Toronto
Hamlyn House, Feltham, Middlesex, England

Copyright © George Every 1970
Second impression 1973
ISBN 0 600 31601 7
Filmset by Filmtype Services Ltd., Scarborough
Manufactured in the United States of America

Contents

Qualiter Abraham iubente deo summa obe-
dientia sacrificare filium suum unicum uo-
lens, iam eleuato gladio ut feriret. ab angelo
retrahitur. et aries pter spem oblatus sacrifi-
tio substituitur.

Quomodo excitus Regis Elamitarum cali-
...onum trium regum. Victo rege gomorre cu
aliis quatuor regibus. captiuos ducunt. zint
alios Loth nepotem habebat.

II

A page from the Maciejowski Old Testament of the thirteenth century. It was presented by a papal mission in 1608 to the Shah Abbas of Persia, who ordered a translation in Persian to be added so that he might have the pleasure of reading it. On the upper panels can be seen, left, the drunkenness of Noah and on the right the Tower of Babel. The lower panel shows Abraham and Isaac on the left, and the Jews taken off to captivity on the right.

Introduction

The word *myth* is used of tales concerning wonders performed by gods and heroes, especially those recited on public occasions such as festivals. It is also used in an extended sense of a story told to throw light on a mystery that cannot be explained. Where all myth is interpreted in this second sense, as it is in some cultures, an antithesis develops between poetry and history, myth and fact, but not necessarily to the disadvantage of poetry. Plato disapproved of poets generally, but concluded his diatribe against the poetry generally accepted in his time with the myth of Er, who came back from the dead with a vision of judgement. Aristotle in his *Poetics* (c. 9) said that 'poetry is more philosophical and more serious than history'.

The disparagement of myth in our own civilisation arises partly from objections to idolatry, which made the early Christians prefer to use some other word, such as mystery or enigma, when they took account of the kind of experience that in other religions gives rise to a myth. This objection was intensified at the Reformation, not only among Protestants but among Catholics in reaction against the revival of classical mythology in the Renaissance. It has been reinforced by the prestige of science, which leads us to make our own myths in scientific terms, and then to read the myths of others as if they were unsuccessful shots at the solution of scientific or meta-physical problems. But as Professor Evans-Pritchard has pointed out in some perceptive comments on Lévy-Bruhl's theories of 'primitive mentality', all field anthropologists agree that those who live on the primitive level spend most of their time dealing with practical affairs in an empirical manner, 'either without the least reference to super-sensible . . . in-fluences, and actions, or in a way in which these have a subord-inate and auxiliary role'.

In their own field of competence modern savages are, and the men of the Middle Ages were, as scientific and inventive as modern civilised men, but they take for granted a difference between this kind and the kind of insight that gives rise to myth. The extension of our field of competence, and the increasing inter-play of theories of knowledge with practical engineering, have no doubt made this difference more com-plex, and the distinction between myth and science more difficult to draw at the critical point, but as we shall see the division has always been difficult.

Myth in tribal religion

One possible approach to the sources of mythology is the consideration of the structure of human society, and in particular the extended family. Through the long hunting and food-gathering stage in prehistory the extended family must have been the basic unit, larger or smaller according to cir-cumstances. It has remained important down to the present day, not only among Bushmen and Australian aborigines, but in conservative civilised societies such as the old Chinese empire. In such societies the terms of kinship are complicated and important. In some Australian tribes, so long as they retained their own institutions, the possibilities of marriage

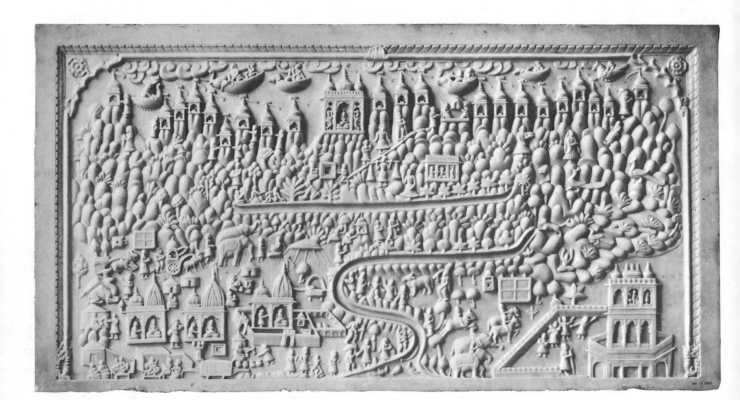

were determined within very narrow limits by tables, not only of prohibited degrees, but of prescribed partners. In such a world the impulse to classify all that bears upon human life, and some things that do not, in terms of relationship to us is strong. Even now in our own scientific terms we class plants and animals by genera and species, by clans and families.

The impulse to classification is found in very primitive conditions, as anthropologists have discovered. American Indians and pygmies know the flora and fauna of their immediate neighbourhood very thoroughly, whether it is of use to them or not, though not exactly in our way. They are aware of relationships between the plants and animals and ourselves and other powers in heaven and earth, rocks and streams and rivers, sun, moon and stars, winds that blow and unseen spirits that move to cheer or to haunt us. Stories told to illustrate these relationships are myths.

Many such stories are told again and again in a variety of changing forms. They gain authority through the repetition of episodes that become essential to their completeness. We all know how children remember and resent an omission from a well-known tale, and fellow tribesmen are much the same. Nevertheless, new dreams give rise to fresh myths in men and women with particular insights. Their powers may be deliberately cultivated by shamans and wizards, who go into a trance

Symbolic representation of a Jain holy place. It gives us some of the feeling of endless repetition that we have in the Hindu symbol of the wheel—the eternal cycle. Carved marble of the nineteenth century. Victoria and Albert Museum.

Above right:
Four panels from an ivory casket of the early fifth century. They display in continuous narrative Pilate washing his hands, Christ carrying his cross, the suicide of Judas Iscariot, the crucifixion and resurrection of Christ, and the doubt and conviction of St Thomas. Maskell Collection, British Museum.

Right:
Satan tempting Christ to make stones into bread, to cast himself down from the pinnacle of the Temple, and to receive the kingdom of the world as the tempter's vassal. From folio 18 in Cotton MSS Nero c. iv, of the twelfth century. British Museum.

13

and return with a tale belonging not to yesterday or tomorrow, but outside time: 'As it was in the beginning, is now and ever shall be for ever and ever.'

Mircea Eliade, in his emphasis on the special experience of the initiated seer, may be generalising from the Siberian peoples whose shamans he has studied intensively, but in his book *Myth and Reality* he has put his finger on something very primitive that is important for later developments, the sense experienced by some shamans, wizards or witch-doctors of withdrawal from this present life into a universe with a different time-scale. In this universe the myths, or rather the relationships expressed in and through the myths, are felt to be literally and factually true, but it is also true that they cannot be described in our universe and in our scale of time, except by means that are inadequate to express their full meaning as experienced by those who have been in that other and different world. In this way stories about the gods in the heavenly places come to be told and explained in a manner that allows of a difference in kind between their kind of truth and an ordinary story about a hunt or a fight, or about men and animals generally.

This distinction is not made consistently or continuously in any society that we should describe as primitive. At the same time it would be a mistake to suppose that such sophisticated

14

peoples as the Egyptians, the Babylonians or the Greeks took
their mythology literally until they became aware of inconsis-
tencies to be explained away. The Egyptians at any rate were
well aware of these and seem to have taken a positive pleasure
in their juxtaposition, as may be seen in some of their art. The
Babylonian priests adapted their rites and myths to fresh
political situations, not with any idea of deception, for no one
would be deceived, but because they fully realised that these
were symbols expressing collaboration between societies of
men on earth and gods in heaven. This collaboration continued, not only through change in the seasons, but through
political change. It was indeed the means whereby such change
was effected. The gods gave victory to a particular city, and
might in course of time bring doom to the same. It was therefore assumed that when Babylon conquered other cities and
captured their gods, these gods had become satellites to

Marduk, the divine king of Babylon. They were summoned to attend his ceremonies and carried in his train. The way in which their submission was expressed in ritual and song was indeed a human invention, but one that might claim divine inspiration.

Myth in the world's religions

Fresh problems arose as peoples became aware of each others' gods, not as conquerors and conquered, but as neighbours living together in the same world, and sometimes subject to the same political controls, with different religions and different laws. Two kinds of response to this situation are possible. They are not incompatible, and may be followed simultaneously, but it is probably true to say that one has always more emphasis than the other. One is to insist on the sacred truth of one's own myth and divine law, pouring scorn on everything else, and the other to allow that all are imperfect, symbolic

The transfiguration of Christ, with John, Peter and James represented as visionaries confounded by the light, while Moses and Elijah are part of the vision. Mosaic of the sixth century at St Catharine's on Sinai.
Left:
Coming out of the Ark. The lion requires help in this mosaic of the thirteenth century in St Mark's Cathedral, Venice.

representations of a mysterious reality, although some are
more distorted than others. The first approach is characteristic
of the Jews, and to a lesser extent of the Greeks and the
Chinese, who regarded other nations are barbarians. It leads to
a closer connection between myth and history, between stories
of gods and stories of ancestors, heroes and kings. So Greek
mythology merged with epic poetry, Chinese with the history
of the foundation of the empire and Jewish with a holy history
containing some very realistic narratives about ordinary human
beings, set in particular places that could be identified. The
second approach emphasises the imperfection of myth as a
vehicle to express the unseen mystery that alone is truly real,
and leads to a philosophical interpretation, in the *Upanishads*,
of the heroic poetry and magical spells in the Indian *Vedas*,
and also to allegorical readings of Homer and other Greek
poets, and of the Bible, in whole or in part.

It is broadly true to say that the West has advanced on the
first path and the East on the second. The history in some of
the *Vedas* has been vindicated by recent archaeological discoveries, but Hindu India is not interested in history but in
eternal meaning, and this is also true of Buddhism. The role of
myth in developed Hinduism, and in the later Buddhism of
the Mahayana, is rather to provide an exercise in envisaging
what would be impossible in this world, and so to dissolve our
attachment to the illusion that our present kind of existence is
real. Christianity on the other hand, which developed out of
Judaism as Buddhism did out of Hinduism, is a more historical
religion than Judaism itself or the other world religion,
Islam, which has also grown out of a Judaeo-Christian background. The Law and the Koran are revelations given to seers
with prophetic gifts, but the heart of the Christian religion is
not the Bible, but the death and resurrection of Christ.

In what sense the resurrection is a historical event is a
matter of debate, to which we shall return in due course, but
the death of Christ belongs unmistakeably to a particular
historical context. In the reign of Tiberius Caesar, while
Pontius Pilate was governor of a small province called Judaea,
Jesus of Nazareth was executed by crucifixion outside the walls
of Jerusalem. This event and the strange complex of events
that followed it, called by Christians the resurrection, the
ascension, and the coming of the Holy Spirit, has become an
occasion of seasonal celebration, year by year from Easter
to Whitsun, week by week on Friday, Saturday and Sunday.
It has acquired the quality of a timeless myth for those who
believe that the man who was crucified then and there is alive
for evermore.

The Christian myth

The Christian Church came to maturity among poor, humble
people with little workshops in the back streets of Levantine
cities, and among peasants and fisherfolk in Syrian and
Anatolian villages. In these surroundings it was perfectly
natural that the story of Christ's life, of his birth, ministry and
death, should be told in the manner of myths of the gods,
with colours heightened, and dark and light intensified. No
Christian, no one of any religion, and very few informed

A mosaic originally conceived as a symbolic representation of the transfiguration. Christ is the cross on the sphere, flanked by law and prophecy. The three sheep below are Peter, James and John. The twelve below are probably apostles, but the twelve above may be angels. St Apollinaris at the bottom is an interpolation, for which a miraculous explanation had to be found. The original design is almost certainly of the sixth century. The mosaic is in the apse of St Apollinare in Classe, outside Ravenna.
Below:
Inspiration: St Matthew listening to an angel as to a muse. His scroll begins with 'the book of the generations', very like the genealogies of Anglo-Saxon kings, some of which are certainly pre-Christian. This is in the Codex Aureus, a sixth or seventh-century illuminated manuscript which seems to have once been in England, and is now in the Royal Library at Stockholm.
Left:
Bronze figure of the Egyptian Ra, enthroned as king over the pyramid, with the sun over his falcon's head and his sceptre shared between sun and falcon. It shows considerable sophistication in the choice and use of symbolism. Twenty-second dynasty. British Museum.

students of religious history will doubt that there were healings, not only of the possessed, the demoniacs of the Gospels, but of some who were blind, lame or paralysed, and others who at any rate appeared to be dead. But these miracles may well have been multiplied, and some parables of what should happen may have been turned into wonder stories of what did happen. The virgin birth, like the resurrection, needs distinct consideration.

It is important for us to realise that for those who believed in the pre-existence of souls (and as we shall see Jews held this belief as well as Gentiles) there was always a problem about the relation between this and conception. What part did sexual intercourse play in compelling souls to be born?

Where there was no compulsion, but a will to encounter the perils of human life, a virgin birth might well be considered more natural. Many believed that Plato had been so conceived, and that vultures seen soaring between earth and heaven and feeding on flesh conceived without copulation. In any case the first apostolic proclamation was of participation in Christ's death and resurrection, of the possibility of dying to rise again in his risen body. It was important therefore to insist that Christ's flesh after the resurrection was seen and felt, that it was not an apparition but the beginning of the transformation of man for union with God in the resurrection. Further pursuit of the implications of this argument made it as important to insist that Christ was truly born in the flesh and really died on the cross, that his life and death were much more than the manifestation of a divine being under human appearances, but rather a real incarnation of the Son of God in a human soul and body. The virgin birth then came into its own, but with as much emphasis on the reality of the birth as on the virginity of Mary. In the Roman rite of baptism the questions asked of the candidate are still substantially those that were asked in the third century. The second is: 'Do you believe in Jesus Christ, His only Son, our Lord, who was born into the world and suffered for us?'

Here we have an insistence on the historical reality of Jesus, a human being in whom the Son of God was born and died and rose again; an insistence that is older than the choice of books to form the canon of the New Testament. But they are not therefore free from the element of myth.

The clearest instance of this is the story of the temptation of Christ by Satan in the wilderness, a story that could have been told by Jesus himself, or created out of a number of his own references to his trials and temptations. The order of the temptations is different in *St Matthew* and *St Luke,* but clearly derived from a common source, to which a brief reference is made in *St Mark.* The temptation is evidently conceived as a visionary experience, in which demons, angels and beasts are involved, the normal material of myth. The transfiguration is more of a borderline case, in that it is recounted as a waking vision of three of the apostles, in which they saw historical characters conversing with Christ in glory and heard a voice from heaven. In both cases there is a characteristic irruption of the timeless into time, of the sort that normally gives rise to a fresh myth, but the transfiguration is of a historical person speaking to historical people, who are also addressed by the voice of God. It exemplifies the unique character of Christian mythology that in it the experience of eternity is also an experience of history; but history mythologised in being celebrated. The choice of Moses and Elijah to represent prophecy and the law may well have been determined by their mysterious disappearances, Moses into the mists of Pisgah, Elijah in his chariot of fire, so that no one knew the grave of either.

On the other hand there are elements in all four Gospels, and in the *Acts of the Apostles,* that have nothing symbolical or mythical about them. They are interesting simply because

The temptation and the fall. At the top on the left Eve converses with the snake. On the right she offers the fruit to Adam. In the centre they are ashamed and hide their privy parts. Below an angel blows a trumpet of doom and another pushes them out of the garden. From a twelfth-century copy of the Homilies of James Kokkinobaphos, Greek MS 1208 in the Bibliothèque Nationale, Paris.

ρίαςδιαφωτϛ
ωρίαμαμ̇ΤΗ·

Jesus Christ or the apostles were concerned in them. This does not necessarily give them a more reliable historical actuality than that of the appearances of Christ after his resurrection. The evidence for some of these, and for some of his words and actions at his last supper before his arrest and death, is certainly older, and probably more secure, than the evidence of the *Acts of the Apostles* about St Paul's relations with the apostles at Jerusalem. This is in conflict, at any rate in some places, with the older evidence of St Paul's letters. It would seem that some frictions have been smoothed over and some episodes omitted, but this is not myth. It has more to do with the eirenic bias characteristic of the kind of church historian who dislikes giving occasions for scandal.

Scripture and legend

The canon, or complete list of books, of the Old Testament was not finally fixed by the synagogue until the end of the first century A.D. For this and for other reasons the early Church followed the *Septuagint,* the Greek version of the Old Testament used in many synagogues of the Jewish dispersion, from which a large number of church members came. Much later, in the fourth and fifth centuries, St Jerome used the Hebrew for his new translation into Latin, but the books in the *Septuagint* that are omitted from the final revision of the Hebrew Bible remain in the Bible of the Roman Catholic and Eastern Orthodox churches, though the churches of the Reformation consider them apocryphal. The canon of the New Testament also had a slow growth. By the middle of the second century the superiority of four Gospels over others was generally recognised, and the accepted collection of St Paul's Epistles was like our own. But some of the other letters at the end of the New Testament, such as the *Epistle to the Hebrews* and the *Revelation of St John,* took time to win recognition, and other books were included in bibles in the fourth and fifth centuries.

Reasons for the choice of books were complex in both cases. It is true, and relevant for our purposes, that the rejected books of the Old and New Testaments contained a great deal in the way of visionary materials, and many extravagant stories. But I do not think that this was the main reason for their rejection. *The Book of Daniel,* or part of it, was included in the Old Testament both in the Hebrew and in the Greek *Septuagint,* when other apocalyptic literature of the same kind was left out, probably because the compilers really believed that these were Daniel's visions in the time of Cyrus and Darius, whereas most other apocalypses were ascribed to impossibly ancient authors.

In a similar way the *Apocalypse of St John* was included in the New Testament, because the Asiatic churches were agreed in ascribing it to the apostle St John himself, or to some other early disciple with the same name, while the *Apocalypse of St Peter* and his first and second letters gave rise for more doubt. Were they by the apostle himself or later compositions? In the end the letters were accepted, but not the apocalypse, which modern critics connect with the second letter. Both of these are certainly later than the apostle's time.

Left:
Symbols of the four evangelists around a sphere
bearing the Chi-Rho monogram of Christ, with
four angels between them. From left to right
we read St John's eagle, the flying lion of St
Mark, St Luke's ox, and the most human
and historical 'figure of a man', St Matthew.
The idea is derived from *Revelation* 4. 7. The
mosaic is in the Oratory of St Andrew in the
Archbishop's palace at Ravenna and could be of
the sixth century or earlier.
Right:
An early form of the so-called 'Tree of Jesse'.
David's father stands at the foot flanked by
Moses at the burning bush and Gideon watching rain (*pluvia*) not dew (*ros*) descend upon his
fleece (*vellus*) and on the dry ground (*Judges* 6.
37–40). The Virgin is called by her Greek title,
and the whole may well be derived from a
Greek model. It may be significant that her
proffered breast does not disturb the lines of
her dress in any way and is yet a powerful
symbol, as is the Child's hand raised in blessing.
Above her stands the Dove of the Holy Spirit
between two more symbols of salvation, Daniel
in the den of lions and the three young men in
the fiery furnace (*Daniel* 3). In a Cistercian
lectionary made at Cîteaux, where the order
was founded, before 1120, but now at Dijon in
the municipal library.

On the first letter, which was more readily accepted by the
early Church, opinions still differ.

What is important is that the early Church was much
concerned with authentic witness to the early life and death
of Jesus Christ, and to the earliest, formative stages of the
Church's life in the Holy Spirit, but this could include
experience embodied in myth. The Church was very much
concerned with what Christ had to say of the coming end of
the world, and yet this was recognised as mysterious symbolic
language, like that in the prophets and apocalyptic writings,
about present history and future catastrophe. Prophecy of
this sort has continued through the history of the Church,
in the West into the Middle Ages, and in the East more
recently, and has been judged by comparison with the
scriptural accounts.

The gulf between scripture and legend widened in the West
towards the end of the Middle Ages, first of all because the
rules of scholastic debate on matters of doctrine heightened
the emphasis on the primacy of the literal or historical sense of
any passage in the Bible that might be cited in support of an

argument. Until then the whole Bible had been treated as open to the kind of multiple interpretation that had been applied to Egyptian and Greek myths, and then to the Old and New Testaments, by scholars in the tradition of the Alexandrian schools. The mystical interpretation of scripture, like the interpretations of the *Vedas* in the *Upanishads,* had small regard to the literal sense, and often extended the scope of myth where it was out of place. But mystical interpretation did at least prevent Jews and Christians from turning all their myths into literal history.

After a thousand years – in the fourteenth century – it began to fall into disrepute, largely because of the difficulty of deciding, in a scholastic disputation on a point of doctrine, between rival mystical interpretations of the same text. Nevertheless the spiritual sense remained important, and it continued to colour approaches to the Bible until after the Reformation. Controversy then became more actual, and disputation more fierce.

But it was the Renaissance rather than the Reformation which cast a blight on the fertile growth of legend, of what we might call subsidiary mythology on secondary themes, the lives of Mary and the saints, the legendary history of relics and of the cross. The Renaissance established a hard line between apostolic tradition (for Protestants in scripture alone) and unreliable legend, classical and Christian.

Scripture and history

The new situation appears most clearly in the seventeenth century, when many myths that had passed for a kind of history were quickly discredited. In Britain the mythical history of Brut, who came from Troy and landed at Totnes, and of a long line of British kings including Cymbeline and Lear was history no longer. King Arthur and his knights followed them into the shadows. Milton, who had intended to write an epic about them, wrote one instead on creation and the fall, Adam and Eve and the serpent, Satan in conflict with Christ. He was too good a poet not to recognise the poetical character of much of this material, and he treated it with an original poet's freedom. Nevertheless he believed it to be true in a different sense from King Arthur and Queen Guenevere, the Holy Grail and the Round Table. An older contemporary of his, Archbishop Ussher of Armagh, provided the margins of the authorised version of the Bible with dates that we still see there. For a little time holy scripture, acknowledged as authoritative by Roman Catholic and Puritan alike, appeared superior in every kind of truth, including historical truth, to any kind of legend; but it was still recognised as myth in that no difficulty arose through multiple and irreconcilable accounts of the same event in *I Samuel* or in the Gospels. They were as natural and inevitable as the diversity of faces, buildings, colours in representations of Biblical scenes.

This could not last for long. Historical criticism was an inevitable consequence of the exaltation of the historical and literal sense of scripture over the mystical and moral. In the East, where this had not happened, the impact was delayed.

Mystical theology was more alive on Mount Athos in the eighteenth century, when the great collections of monastic theology were compiled there, than in any Western monastery, but in the West where the Greek Fathers were read the impact was less severe.

The spread of Western scholastic methods in the schools brought scholastic questions, but these could be countered by appeals to an older tradition of mystical interpretation.

In Protestant Christendom the threat to the foundations of doctrine was not only more direct, for the Reformation appealed to the Bible against all other tradition, but far more difficult to control than in the churches under Rome. In the course of the nineteenth century the Protestant appeal began to be to the history in the Bible, rather than to the text of the Bible itself. The historical critic began to displace the scholastic theologian as an arbiter of doctrine, not only among Protestants, for Roman Catholic defences were affected by the new look in Protestant controversy.

Myths and their translation

That there are myths in the Bible would now be admitted by nearly everyone. Probably all Roman Catholics and a majority of Protestants would hold that the account of creation in *Genesis* 1 and 2 is mythical in form, though some would attach great importance to the descent of the whole human species from a single pair of ancestors. Most Christians would also admit that the story of Eve's temptation is a myth as it stands, influenced by other and older mythological materials. Belief that man is a fallen creature in no way depends on the factual truth of this story. Few would maintain the literal truth of any passage in the *Revelation of St John,* a book whose symbolic quality has been recognised in every age of Christian history, and all would allow that any description of the descent into hell must be mythological. To remove all mythology from the Bible would impoverish the text, and in many places destroy the significance of historical passages which are not history in our sense, but part of the myth whose function is to complete and support it.

If myths are not to be removed they must be translated, but they cannot be interpreted until they are understood. This book and other books on comparative mythology may contribute something to this. I have written on creation, the flood and the end of history as they are seen through the Bible, and also on the stories of the fall. After this I have taken a strange road through a maze of legend linking the grave of Adam with the death and resurrection of Christ. There are episodes in Hebrew history that were as mythology to the medieval Church – Israel's enslavement in Egypt, the crossing of the Red Sea, and crises in the lives of David and Solomon – but it is difficult to consider them today except in the light of historical criticism, which distinguishes between the history and the legend in them. This is a valuable exercise, with a religious importance for those who believe in the historical character of the Christian myth, even if the importance of establishing the historicity of particular details is often exaggerated. But it is out of place in a book about myths.

'The end of the silver age'. The immediate reference is to a passage in Hesiod's *Works and Days* (136–40), which was used to interpret the long lives of the patriarchs between the fall and the flood in terms of babies who played with their mothers for a hundred years before growing up to be brazen brutes. The painter, Lucas Cranach the Elder (1472–1553) was a friend of Luther, employed by his patron, Frederick the Wise, and no doubt regarded this as a transition from the state of innocence to the bondage of the will after the fall. National Gallery, London.

Left:
Birth and death are an endlessly recurring cycle
in Hindu belief. A remarkable expression of
this can be seen in the construction of the
great sun temple to Vishnu-Surya at Konarak
in Orissa, which has the shape of a great solar
chariot borne on twelve wheels. Each wheel is
ten feet in diameter, and the wheel is the
symbol of the eternal cycle. Thirteenth
century.
Far right:
This stained glass window is chiefly concerned
with the life and miracles of the Virgin Mary,
and with her interpreters and admirers.
In the left-hand lancet we may see a
burning house (first on left) put out by St
Gregory of Tours (c. 600), with a reliquary
containing possessions of the Blessed Virgin
(first on right). St Bernard of Clairvaux, who
did much to advance devotion to her though he
did not believe in her immaculate conception,
is second on the left. The other figures in the
left lancet are illustrated below. The whole is of
the thirteenth century in the Lady Chapel at
Le Mans Cathedral.
Right:
These details are all from the bottom of the
left-hand lancet, and illustrate a story told by
St Gregory of Tours about some columns,
probably from a pagan temple, intended to be
used in building a church for the Blessed
Virgin. These could not be shifted (left) until
on her instructions two schoolboys did it (top).
The lady on the right is said to be Esther going
to plead with King Ahasuerus (*Esther* 4 and 5),
an appropriate figure of the Virgin's interces-
sion. The money changers below are the donors
of the window.

As things are at present, I find myself faced with as great or
greater difficulties in any consideration of myth in the New
Testament. Here more than anywhere else myth and history
overlap, but anyone who treats the four Gospels in their
mythical aspects is liable to be charged with trying to remove
the myths or to treat them as inaccurate records of events.
Therefore while it is quite impossible to omit the Gospels
altogether in an account of Christian mythology, I have given
more space to Apocryphal Gospels, Acts and Apocalypses
whose legendary nature is not seriously contested. Here the
growth of myth throws light on history, and sometimes a
consideration of developing mythology may even bring to light
a historical fact, insecurely attached to a growing myth.

The same considerations apply to much in the lives of the
saints. Visions of the afterlife by their nature must be myths,
but they more than any others raise the question of our need
for some mythology if we believe in any kind of immortality. I
have taken them from a variety of sources in different periods
and places, and have made no attempt to impose uniformity.
Nevertheless I hope that a pattern may emerge that could be
of some use to Christians in our day, and in the last chapter
but one I have tried to draw some implications. The last
chapter is concerned chiefly with sources and may serve as an
introduction to other materials.

25

Creation, flood and fall

Many myths of first beginnings are connected with seasonal rituals, celebrating the dawn of a new year, determining the right and wrong days to do the accustomed things in the coming season according to a calendar. We know, for instance, that the Babylonian myth of creation was recited as part of the action in a new year festival. At this festival the creation of the world and the foundation of the city and empire of Babylon were celebrated in rites commemorating the victory of the god Marduk over the monster Tiamat, his release from prison inside the ziggurat, the holy mountain of Babylon, and his marriage with the goddess Ishtar in a bridal bed at the summit of the mountain. Destinies were determined and a calendar

Left:
Mesopotamian seal showing a god coming out of a mountain. It relates to an earlier form of the spring festival ritual than the one that is more fully documented in its late Babylonian forms. The waters are identified by fishes, the fields by stooks made up of sheaves of corn. The god himself carries a sickle and the flying wind-god or goddess who welcomes him a fan to wave for a good wind. Akkadian of about 2500 B.C. British Museum.

Left below:
A Babylonian cylinder seal showing a worshipper between a god and a goddess, probably Marduk and Ishtar. The emblem above the worshipper is that of the god Asshur.

Right:
God taking Eve out of Adam on the right and giving her pastoral direction on the left. From Genesis A, an eleventh-century copy of an earlier Anglo-Saxon paraphrase probably written in Northumbria in the eighth century and illustrated in this way in Wessex in the MSS Junius 11, f. 9 in the Bodleian Library, Oxford.

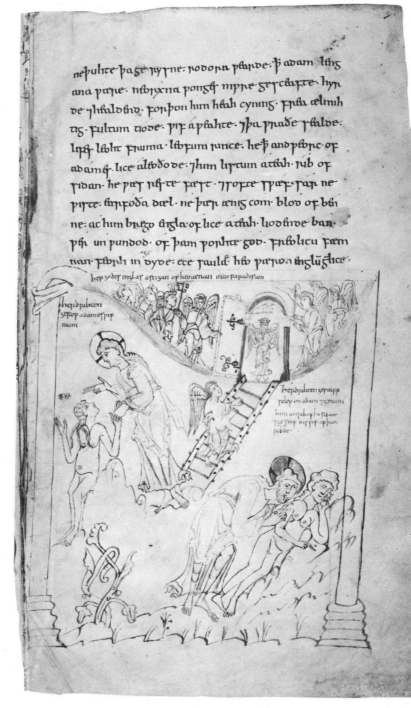

fixed for the rest of the year after a procession in which all the gods of the subject cities were represented by their images.

It is a moot question how far this pattern was commonly followed in Mesopotamia and Syria. Those who have laid most stress on a common type of myth and ritual everywhere have been attacked for ignoring differences between Mesopotamia and Egypt, where seasonal festivals were rather connected with a periodic renewal of the royal power, as well as for under-estimating the altogether peculiar elements in the religion of Israel. It is by no means certain that the myths of creation in *Genesis* 1 and 2 were ever recited at a new year festival in Solomon's Temple at Jerusalem. But one of them is recited at the Paschal vigil, the oldest part of the Easter festival, itself the oldest feast of the Christian Church, and both are associated with the beginnings of preparation for Lent and Easter at Septuagesima. The story of the flood and of new beginnings after that first great catastrophe is read in the same sequence of lessons before Lent, and used to be read on Easter night. This, and the second creation story that fills the greater part of *Genesis* 2, are in their present form older than the first story at the very beginning of the Bible. They may never have been part of a Jewish rite, but they contain material belonging to a type of myth very closely connected with rituals to promote the fertility of the soil.

The second creation story

The creation story in *Genesis* 2.4-25 begins 'In the day the Lord made the earth and the heavens'. No account of their creation is given, but this could have been eliminated in the conflation of the two stories. The earth was dry and hard without a blade of grass, but a mist or a flood came up from underneath and made it all soft before God made man, the first living thing, from the dust of the earth turning to mud and slime. He formed him from the clay and 'breathed into his nostrils the breath of life'. A Christian transposition of this is in one of a number of eucharistic prayers of thanksgiving in a missal found at the Abbey of Reichenau. The leaves of the missal had been used for other writing at the end of the seventh century. The texts may be of the fifth century:

'In the chaos of confused beginnings and the everlasting darkness of floating objects you imposed wonderful forms on the wondering elements, when the young world blushed at the sun's fire and the raw earth marvelled at the moon's business. That all this might not be uninhabited and an empty space to serve only things, your hands fashioned a figure of clay, animated with holy fire, as the swift spirit quickened the slow parts. The inwardness of this, O Father, we are not allowed to examine. You only know the greatness of your work, how human limbs first stirred as the earth began to move and the blood in the veins to flow, and as the body was freed the nerves came into action, and the bones about the inner organs grew strong. Why should we be given such gifts, the wretches that we are? We are made like you and your Son, and from lumps of clay made into eternal beings. But we forgot the commands of your blessedness and, being mortal, sank again into the earth from whence we came. We wept, having lost

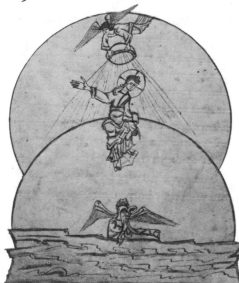

The creation of light from Genesis A. MSS 11, f. 6 in the Bodleian Library, Oxford.
Left:
The Ark is ready and God prepares to shut the door, as in *Genesis* 7. 16. But Noah's wife is still reluctant to come up the stairs. From Genesis A, in MSS Junius 11, f. 66 in the Bodleian Library, Oxford.

the eternal comfort of your presence.'

In a Spanish prayer of the same sort, and rather later: 'You make man without any trouble on your part, for your generosity does it, without any burden of necessity. Your glorious hands work the mud and impose on slime the image of Godhead, shape the face, part the members. With the breath of your lips you blow and quicken the soul with reason, who comes out from your side.'

In the same soft ground God planted a garden of fruit trees, and set down man to be the gardener. In this version of the story the animals and birds come later. Each of them, one by one, was brought to man and given a name, but not one of them could help with the gardening work. His helper had to be formed from his own flesh and bone, by taking a rib from him as he slept. This image is perhaps a deliberate variation on the more natural one of a bisexual human being giving birth to a son. There is no idea of creation out of nothing, but there is an idea of man's domination over all the beasts of the field and birds of the air. In naming the animals he takes them into his world, which henceforth is the world of man according to God's purpose for him. And he is in charge of the garden, free to eat the fruit of any tree but one.

The flood and Noah's Ark

The story of the Ark is more like this than will appear at first sight. This is a tale of a new beginning, a new age emerging after a great catastrophe. The whole world of living flesh was going to be destroyed, as we sometimes think may happen in nuclear warfare, but Noah was warned. He and his wife, his sons and their wives and families, with two of every sort of living creature (or in another version seven pairs of some and one each of others) were to be saved by entering an 'ark' made for the purpose by Noah himself, with supplies of food stored in it. The same word is used for the 'ark' of bullrushes in which Moses, as a baby, was set to float on the Nile, before he was rescued by Pharaoh's daughter. In the Greek Bible, but not in the Hebrew, the same word is used for the Ark of the Covenant, the box containing Israel's sacred objects.

We all know how the story of Noah's ark can be played, for many of us have played it as children. It is not difficult to imagine a dry deck or platform, like the earth envisaged in the second story of creation. This might be flooded from above or beneath. The bronze 'sea' in Solomon's Temple stood upon twelve metallic oxen, all looking out from underneath. These were probably models for the living creatures who carried the flying platform, 'the likeness of a firmament shining like crystal', in the vision of Ezekiel (2. 22). On this platform the throne of God was standing, with God himself enthroned upon it in human form. It may be that in this sea an ark was floated and filled with human and animal figures as required for a rain-making ritual, or at a festival of creation a representative man might interview one by one a number of animals, and then the right woman. The object of such a rite would be to celebrate man's dominion over the rest of nature and his special relationship with God, with woman, and with at least some of the animals.

This is clearly set forth at the end of the story of the flood, when God blessed Noah and his sons: 'The fear and dread of you shall be with every beast of the earth and bird of the air, with everything that creeps on the ground and every fish in the sea. All are delivered into your hands.' All living things and plants shall be food for men, but they may not 'eat with the blood'. The blood, which is the life, must be poured out on to the earth, the source of life. On this condition a covenant is made, not only between God and man, but between man and every beast who was with Noah and his children in the ark. 'Never again shall all flesh be cut off by the waters of a flood.' 'While the earth remains, seedtime and harvest, cold and heat, summer and winter, day and night, shall not cease.' The sign of the covenant is the bow in the clouds, the sun shining through rain. This, like the second story of creation, relates to a rite to ensure the return of spring, or more likely the coming of the autumn rains at the end of a long and arid summer. What is distinctively Israelite about it is the election of man as God's chosen people. This can be conceived as a step along the historical road to the election of Israel, but also as significant in itself, since the choice of man to rule the rest of nature determines the human situation for the future, if that choice be accepted as the basis for man's attitude to the world.

God creating Adam. From the central bay of the north portal of Chartres Cathedral, early in the thirteenth century.
Left:
God creating Adam, as represented by Michelangelo in the Sistine Chapel at the Vatican.

The first creation story

The creation story in *Genesis* 1 and 2.1-4a is much more sophisticated. It was probably put into its present form after the return of the Jews from exile in Babylon, at some time in the fifth century B.C. It shows the influence of the Jews' theological concern to insist on the responsibility of their own God for the whole of creation. Reminiscences of ritual actions are still present, and some of them may still have been performed in the restored Temple. At verse 6, for instance, where 'God said: "Let there be a firmament in the midst of the waters"', and at verse 9: 'Let the waters under the heavens be gathered . . . and let the dry land appear': something may have been done at this point to the water in the sea of bronze. But the motive of the arrangement is rather to confirm the dependence of everything on God's unique determination 'in the beginning'. God moved on the waters when they were utterly without form.

The order is important, that we proceed from formless chaos through binary divisions between the light and the dark, the heaven and the earth, the land and the sea, the plants and the trees, the sun and the moon, fishes and birds, beasts and reptiles, finally man and woman. This is an orderly process of development, although the order of events is not as we should put it with our knowledge of the evolution of the species. The perspective is wider and more cosmic than in the second story, the first in time.

As the second story struck the imagination of Christians close to the soil in Gaul and Spain, the first story of creation was understood as myth in civilised places such as the Syrian Antioch, where the *Apostolic Constitutions* were compiled out of earlier texts in the last quarter of the fourth century A.D. These contain two prayers reflecting on creation, one in chapter 34 of Book 7 and another in the eucharistic liturgy of Book 8. The first is the source of the second and depends very closely on older Jewish materials. It contains such passages as:

'How can any man describe the sea? The tide comes in in a rage from the deep, but ebbs and is stayed by mere sand at your command: "Thereby shall her waves be broken". Small and great fish you have made her sustain, and ships afloat on their voyages. At your word the earth also grew green and gay with all sorts of flowers and trees. The stars that nourish these maintain their courses, and never deviate from their appointed ways, but as you bid they rise and set, to be signs of seasons and years, and so of man's changing employments. So too all the varieties of animals, fishes, birds, gulls and amphibious creatures were created and by your foresight given each his own provision.

'And at the end of creation you commanded your Wisdom to make a rational animal, a citizen of the world, saying: "Let us make a man in our own image and after our likeness". As a world within a world you made him, forming his body from the first four elements, but making ready his soul out of non-being, endowed with five senses and with an intelligence to be their steersman.'

Some at least of these prayers in Book 7 reflect the influence

The disaster of Eve: God is pulling a rib out of Adam in the top register on the right, and the results are seen on the left. In the centre God addresses Eve and presents her to Adam on the left, the temptation and fall are concentrated on the right. Below, Adam and Eve are expelled from the garden and on the right are clothed in skins, living under a bower, Adam wielding a primitive hoe and Eve nursing Cain, who in this picture is a large but apparently happy baby. From the Bible of St Calixtus, of about 870, at St Paul-without-the-walls, Rome.

Below:

The temptation and expulsion from Eden as represented with the maximum of concentration by Michelangelo. Note that the serpent has a human head as in the illustration from St Augustine, and that Adam picks the fruit for himself while Eve receives it from the tempter. In the Sistine Chapel at the Vatican.

of Philo, the Alexandrian Jew of the first century A.D. who combined Rabbinic learning with Platonic philosophy. Philo certainly made a very clear distinction between the heavenly man in the image of God who was made in *Genesis* 1 and his mortal embodiment fashioned out of clay in the second story of creation. The heavenly man is an idea in the Platonic sense, an archetype, a real kind, neither masculine nor feminine, in his sublime nature incorruptible and immortal. Mortal man is a compound of earthly elements with this divine spirit blown into him. The first Adam was indeed superior to all his descendants in beauty and stature. He was free from all disease and affliction, possessed extraordinary powers of perception, and had converse with the angels in heaven, but while he lived a long time, and would have lived longer if he had not fallen, he was by nature mortal. Philo was too much of a Platonist to think immortality of the body desirable. In his eyes the immortality of the soul is our participation in the heavenly man.

The primal man

What looks like a reference to the heavenly man appears in *Ezekiel* 28.13–15 as part of an oracle against Tyre: 'You were in Eden, the garden of God; every precious stone was your

covering . . . on the holy mountain of God; in the midst of
the stones of fire you walked'. This is a fragment, centuries
before Philo, but *The Book of the Secrets of Enoch* has been
held to have some connection with Alexandrian Judaism. It
survives only in a Slavonic version, but the original was
certainly pre-Christian. In this we are told that man was made
out of seven substances; his flesh from the earth, his blood
from the dew, his eyes from the light of the sun, his bones
from the stones, his thought from the swiftness of angels and
clouds, his veins and his hair from the grass of the earth, his
spirit from the wind and the Spirit of God. He had bones for
endurance and sweetness for thought. He was a second angel,
a ruler of all the earth. God gave him free will, and showed
him the two ways of light and darkness, calling them good and
evil, but he sinned through ignorance of his own nature, and
God 'appointed death on account of his sin'. But a little later
we are told that God 'made him a wife, and by his wife death
came'. This is said to have happened when Satan 'entered and
deceived Eve', but nothing created came to be cursed, neither
man nor the earth, but only his sins and their consequences.

Three views of man's original condition have been read into
the early chapters of *Genesis;* that he was an immortal
and impeccable being, automatically subject to the divine
control in a heavenly place, even if this was on earth; that his
mortal frailty made him subject to decay and so to sin and
error; and that God implanted in him a good and an evil
imagination, with power to choose between them. As late as
the seventeenth century there was much theological dispute
as to his freedom of choice in the state of innocence in matters
morally indifferent, such as which side of the garden should be
hoed this morning, or where to go for a walk. Some held that
man was free in Eden as never before and after, but others
that the fall was from God's complete control to the domination of the devil.

The fall of Eve and Adam
Needless to say, none of these views of determinism or freedom
are supported by the text of *Genesis* 3. But other arguments
about sex and death in the state of innocence are connected
with the details of the story. In the first story of creation man
is made in male and female form or forms. In the second his
flesh and bones are divided in sleep between these forms.
There are also two special trees in the midst of Eden, of life
and of the knowledge of good and evil, and of these the second
is named and forbidden, as poison: 'for in the day that you eat
of it you shall die'. This commandment is given to the man
before the woman is taken out of him. In *Genesis* 3 however
she knows it in another form. It is dangerous to taste or even
to touch the fruit of the tree in 'the midst of the garden', but
the threat of death is not immediate, and she does not know
the tree has to do with knowledge until the serpent tells her.

The serpent in this story is not Satan, but an intelligent
animal, who stands for animate life in general in so far as this
rebels against its own limitations and wants to be God or the
gods. (In mythology he is usually a semi-divine symbol of
fertility, healing and wisdom.) He enquires of the woman

about the conditions of employment in the garden, and so
draws from her the single exception to the general rule that the
fruit is free. He then insists that the fruit of the forbidden tree
is the best. God has forbidden it because he knows that 'when
you eat it, your eyes will be opened, and you will be like God,
knowing good and evil'. Since the serpent is a sinister character, we know that this is a half truth. The forbidden fruit
will communicate some knowledge to the man and the woman,
but in fact this consists in acute embarrassment about the
appearance of their privy parts, which they have to conceal
with the first convenient figleaf. They hear God walking in the
garden in the cool of the day, and skulk behind the trees, but
he calls them out and gets the truth from them, although
Adam blames Eve and Eve the serpent.

In the divine reproaches that followed, the serpent was first
degraded from a figure of intelligence into a thing that creeps
and crawls, trampled by men's feet, but biting back at their
heels. Eve was also condemned to pain in childbirth, intensified by her passion for Adam and her subjection to him. His
penalty was hard work on rebellious soil, the permanent
struggle with recaltricant nature.

This can be taken as a myth of the human condition. Adam
and Eve were like young children in a climate where all tod-
dlers are happiest naked, and quite unembarrassed by their
bodies until they fall into sin by eating forbidden fruit or
doing something else for which they have been threatened
with instant or probable death. They are then found out, and
this is their worst penalty, producing a sense of shame about
everything, and more especially about their naked condition.
Something like this view of the story was taken by a number
of Christian writers towards the end of the second century.
St Irenaeus in particular compared the embraces of Adam and
Eve to those of small boys and girls 'kissing and embracing
each other in purity after the manner of children'. Their sin
lay in breaking a rule that was made for their discipline, but in
any case they had to grow towards perfection from the image
into the likeness of God. St Irenaeus and others who took
similar views no doubt believed in the historical actuality of a
crisis at the beginning of human history, represented to us by
this story, but he thought this crisis was best understood in
terms of its repetition in every boy and girl before Mary, the
'second Eve', who gave birth to the second Adam, the Son of
Man in Christ, through whom the human race had a fresh
start and a second chance.

But there is another way of reading the story, in which the
shame that Eve and Adam developed as a result of their
disobedience is specifically sexual. Man in the image of God
had no sexual differentiation. He might have multiplied fissi-
parously in some mysterious way, but without sin he would
have had no desire for children or for any physical intercourse,
and he would have remained immortal – or at any rate lived as
long as the earth was required for him and his like. Among
those who held this view was St Gregory of Nyssa, one of the
Cappadocian Fathers who had great influence in the Eastern
church from the end of the fourth century. It is interesting to

St Augustine's account in his *City of God* of sin
leading to death as represented in a French MS
of the fifteenth century, 246, f. 241 v., Bibliothèque Ste Geneviève, Paris.

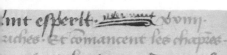

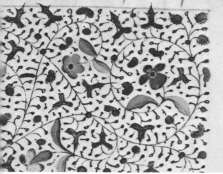

find that he himself was married, and that although he wrote a work in praise of celibacy he could also be eloquent about the married state. His primary concern in his interpretation of Adam was probably to show that the image of God is in woman as well as in man. On the other hand his younger contemporary St Augustine, who believed that in the state of innocence Adam and Eve had no sense of guilt or shame about their sexual life, took a very severe attitude to the 'perturbation' and disturbance which in our fallen state accompany sex. He saw in his own compulsive passions, whose origins he traced in his *Confessions*, the evidence of a condition which he himself was the first to call original sin. It was passion, not sex, that he abhorred, but his own troubles in later life, some of them probably connected with the special relationship between his mother and himself, led him to see all passion in sexual terms and his own passions in babies crying because their wishes were thwarted or out of jealousy of their foster brothers: 'the weakness, not of the will of infant limbs is innocence'. He found his view implied in the practice of infant baptism, for he took this to mean that children are conceived and born in sin and are in urgent need of exorcism. Without baptismal regeneration they are children of wrath from the moment of birth.

In this St Augustine believed himself to be interpreting St Paul, whose sense of sin's compulsion was like his own. But he built too much on the passages in 1. *Corinthians* (15. 22) and *Romans* (5. 12) where St Paul writes that 'In Adam all die', and that 'Sin came into the world through one man, and death through sin'. In the first passage, which is earlier and in some respects clearer, St Paul seems to be contrasting his own view with something like Philo's. Philo contrasted the heavenly image with the natural man who came after him, but St Paul insists that 'the spiritual does not come first, but the natural, and the spiritual afterwards. The first man was from the earth, a man of dust, the second man is from heaven . . . As we have borne the image of the man of dust, we shall also bear the image of the man of heaven', who is Christ. The same contrast is in St Irenaeus, between the child Adam and the mature second Adam, who is Son of Man and Son of God. Philo and St Paul were both Jews of the Dispersion, concerned in their different ways to interpret the Old Testament in the world of Greek civilisation. St Irenaeus was a Greek Christian in the same world at a rather later stage, but he was not only nearer St Paul than St Augustine; he and his like have a more balanced view of the human condition. They see that our long infancy is a reason for our troubled relations with others, beginning with our mothers, and therefore the occasion for the beginning of sin. But that does not mean that we start sinning as soon as we begin to cry. St Augustine's recollections of hating Greek and stealing apples were really nearer the mark than his imaginative reconstruction of his own infancy from his observations of babies, and his persistent feelings for a mother who must have been a remarkable woman.

The two cities

Cain and Abel

Satan addressing the fallen angels, as seen by William Blake in terms of Milton's *Paradise Lost* and his own *Milton*. Victoria and Albert Museum.
Below:
Christ coming up out of hell with David and Solomon on the left, Adam and Eve on the right, rising over broken bars and fetters, a door torn from its hinges, and what is probably a prison cell, in a mosaic of about 1020. Hosios Loukas in Phocis, Greece.

The two young men are commonly taken as representing arable and animal husbandry, but these can hardly be regarded as alternative ways of life before the nomad took his flocks into the wilderness. Mixed farming of some sort is older than nomadic life, and this story seems to come from a community with a field for crops and herds. The contrast is rather between two kinds of sacrifice, of first fruits from the ground and of fat portions of meat about to be eaten. In both the god addressed should give some sign, some omen or token of his acceptance. In Abel's offering the lines ran right on the liver and other entrails of the sacred victim, but Cain's meal did not sizzle as it should. The reason for this was presumably his own hatred and jealousy of his young brother, which may have gone back to the day when Eve rejected him for the new baby; but his fault was revealed in his resentment when Abel's sacrifice was a great success while his was not. He was warned that his sin was 'couching', ready to spring, at the door of his heart, but he refused the divine warning against his own desire, and went on to commit the first murder. Asked for his brother's where-abouts he rages: 'Am I my brother's keeper?'. So he revealed his guilt and was driven out from the ground that had received his brother's blood and would work for him no longer. He became a nomad, a wanderer, instead of an arable farmer, but before long he built a city, and his descendants included not only cattle drovers, but musicians and smiths. The story is presented as the first instance of the working of the evil

imagination which appears again in *Genesis* 6.5 and in other places in the Old Testament. In Rabbinic literature this is a more important source of sin than the fall of Adam. Adam's choice, it is sometimes suggested, was between immortality and knowledge, but afterwards 'the wickedness of man was great' because 'every imagination of the thoughts of his heart was only evil continually'. This evil imagination is connected with marriages between human girls and fallen angels.

Sons of God and daughters of men

The story at the beginning of *Genesis* 6 is now regarded as an unassimilated fragment from an alien myth, but its influence on Jewish and Christian thought has been very great. In this the 'sons of God' were enamoured of 'daughters of men', who bore to them 'men of renown'. In later Jewish exegesis these sons of God descend from Seth, Adam's third and favourite son, and the daughters of men from the evil line of Cain, or sometimes they are just good young men and girls of easy morals. But there can be no doubt that this is originally a story about angels. In one version they came down as a body upon Mount Hermon, where two hundred of them under twenty captains swore to maintain their common purpose of rebellion against God. They then seduced the girls and taught them charms and enchantments, especially the virtues of roots and of switches from particular trees that have always played an important part in witchcraft. Their enchanted ladies bore them children, who soon became enormous and grew up to be supermen whose appetites consumed all that their human cousins had gathered, and then they turned to cannibalism.

The expulsion from Eden depicted on the left-hand side of the bronze doors made for St Bernward at the cathedral of Hildesheim early in the eleventh century (top left and right). Adam needs instruction in wielding a hoe (left), but Eve is feeding her long-limbed child. Cain and Abel offer their sacrifices (above), while the bottom panel (right), shows Cain murdering his brother.

In another version of the story the angels came to earth by divine permission before the flood, when evils were increasing and men were going irretrievably to the bad. They offered to do something to save the situation, but God warned them that if they went to live among men their own inclinations would turn to evil and overcome them. They promised to do everything to sanctify God's holy name, and were allowed to go. They made friends with the women, including one good and intelligent girl who wormed the ineffable name of God out of one of them, and so got away to heaven, where she became the constellation of the Pleiades. But others of the women were in competition for the supplies of rouge and other ornaments provided by Azazel, the most ingenious of the angels, and themselves took the initiative in drawing him and others into more dangerous forms of physical contact. Finally they produced babies, some of whom grew into giants, as in the other tale. The giants included the Emin, the Gibborim, the Anakim, and the Nephilim; at least one, Ashmedai or Asmodeus, was a real devil, who strangled new born children if he was allowed to get at them. His mother was Naamah, the sister of Tubal-cain, who was the first to make intruments of bronze and iron. In this way at least the seed of the fallen angels is linked with the line of Cain, and with the growth of human ingenuity in the direction of power to murder.

The difficulty which in time came to limit the importance of this story for Jewish and Christian thought lies in its place in *Genesis* between the fall and the flood. It could serve as an explanation of the almost total destruction of mankind in

Overleaf:
The Tower of Babel as conceived in terms of the Roman Colosseum by Peter Bruegel, a Protestant Fleming of the early seventeenth century. Kunsthistorische Museum, Vienna.

Noah's time, but in that case it must be assumed that the gigantic children of these monstrous unions of demons with women perished in the flood to the last man. One way of saving the situation was to make the fall of the angels a direct consequence of the creation of man, which inspired them with jealousy. Later in some Christian versions of the story they fell first, and man was created primarily for the purpose of filling up gaps in the angelic host. In either case this made it easier to identify the serpent with Satan.

Another way of dealing with the place of the story in *Genesis* 6 is to make it refer to a process that continued after the flood and is still going on. In many cultures for many centuries

Building the Tower of Babel. Cotton MS Claudius B, iv, f. 19 of the eleventh century. British Museum.

Above left:
The fall of the angels as represented in Genesis A. In the top register an angel is planning to set up his throne in the north of heaven. He wears a crown, but he and his companions have no haloes, and it is sinister that he holds his sceptre in his left hand. In the centre peacock's feathers, the symbols of pride, are being distributed when the Lord God intervenes with three arrows and other artillery, and hurls the rebel angels down into hell's mouth, where Satan lies bound. This is on the third page of MS Junius 11 in the Bodleian Library, Oxford.

43

angelic beings have been suspected of responsibility for children whose features or character appear to be out of the ordinary in some divine or demonic way. This need not involve physical paternity, for belief in the pre-existence of the soul is common to many religions. A large Jewish literature implies belief in a supply or store of souls for future generations, who may be compelled to enter a sperm after this has been formed in the womb, despite their protests against the risks of human life which are specially shown to them by the guardian angels who watch over their destiny. This display may go on night after night until all is forgotten as an angel turns off the light in the baby's head and gives him a light blow on the nose as an immediate preparation for being born, much against his or her inclination. Of the two guardian angels who watch over everyone, at any rate one is the accuser and reporter of evil deeds. In some Jewish literature he is even regarded as responsible for our evil inclinations.

It is easy to see how in this background a difficult child might be regarded as subject to demonic influence and in special need of exorcism, and a really bad one as an incarnate devil. Nevertheless in Christendom the general view seems to have been that the devil, or any devil, is incapable of a proper incarnation, because his presence is destructive of the nature of man. A man or woman may be possessed by a devil, but his child would be a monster, not a human being.

The Tower of Babel

The expectation of such a being was in the air before the birth of Christ, and not only in Jewish circles. To the Christians he is known as anti-Christ, and Jews who feared a false Messiah no doubt identified him with Jesus of Nazareth, but much of the imagery about him is connected with the Babylonian battle between Bel or Marduk and the dragon, the primeval chaos let loose again. The tale of the Tower of Babel has some relation to this. In *Genesis* 11.1–9 the theme of divine jealousy is plain. This is to be suspected in the background material behind the story of the fall, for it does suggest a fear of the increase of human knowledge among the angels, who are 'the gods' in the terms of most religions. This fear has been suppressed or concealed in *Genesis* 2 and 3, but in chapter 11 a divine party, speaking in the plural, comes down in force to obstruct the building of a tower to serve as a ladder from earth to heaven. This they do by making mutual misunderstanding through a confusion of speech, which may include culture and religion. In one way this is another parable of what happens to the young. They are always undertaking common tasks with bricks and mortar or something. These tasks are as often as not beyond their strength, and always beyond their powers of organisation. As soon as this is discovered the groups dissolve in mutual misunderstanding and recrimination. But in another way the Tower of Babel is a figure of cities and empires fallen in ruins, the first of a series of visions of judgement on cities in the Old Testament.

It may be important that in later Jewish legend the building of the tower was the first occasion for the sacrifice of human beings for the sake of a structure. If a man fell to his death it

44

did not matter, but if a brick fell, it might take a year to replace. The women made the bricks; they were not allowed to stop even to have a baby. If one was born, they had to wrap it up in a sheet and go on working with the baby strapped to them. In one way or another this has happened often in the course of human history, where persons have been sacrificed for the acquisition of organised power. In the same legend we are told that the builders shot arrows into the heavens. As these came down bloodstained, they believed that they were inflicting casualties upon the heavenly host, but their mutual misunderstandings soon drove them into war with one another. Much of the tower collapsed into the earth, and some of it was burnt, but the ruin remained. This is the original of Babylon, considered as the city of man doomed to destruction because it is organised for a bid to control history instead of God. Such a rebellion generally involves the return of the dragon – the conquered forces of darkness rising again from beneath the earth, and marks the appearance of the man of sin whose ambition it is to be saluted as God.

Creation in the New Testament

The first chapter of the *Gospel of St John* implies a conception of creation farther removed from agricultural creation myths than anything in *Genesis* 1 or 2. In the first verses of the Old Testament 'the earth was without form and void, and darkness was upon the face of the deep'. But in the prologue to St John nothing was made without the Word, the Reason and the Wisdom of God. Darkness becomes visible, the light shines and nothing can quench it. In either case the work of creation is an ordering. In *Genesis* what God created formless was not intended to remain chaotic, but in the Gospel of St John order is found in it, not imposed upon it. Nevertheless what came into being through the underlying operation of reason, and could not continue without a rational structure, revolted against the light of reason and nature, and according to the New Testament refused to receive the Word made flesh.

The problem in Christianity is more acute than in Judaism because the Christian Church rejected the notion that everything made of matter is inferior to a heavenly archetype or idea of the same thing. This belief was widely current in the first two or three centuries of Christian history, and was indeed taken for granted by important groups of Christians. But they were condemned as deviationists by the main body, who insisted on explaining evil and imperfection by sin in someone, in some rebellion of free beings against God's own intention. It was by no means certain, as we have seen, that they had the Old Testament on their side. They took this stand because the Christ had come in a human body, and promised them participation in his resurrection body, which they believed to be human and in a serious sense physical and material.

This standpoint left plenty of room for demonic as well as human sin, but little for inertia or physical disaster except as a consequence of this, either by mischief or as punishment. A longer view of evolution would have allowed a larger place for freedom in organic and perhaps inorganic matter, but this would have been difficult to conceive in a world where matter

Top:
The crucifixion as represented in a mosaic of about 1020 in the catholicon at Hosios Loukas in Phocis, Greece.
Above:
Revelation 12. The woman gives birth in the bed at the top, as in verse 3. The dragon with all his heads comes after her as in verse 4, and her child is caught up into heaven as in verse 5. The seer on the right sees all as in a vision. A French tapestry of 1375–1400 made by Jean Bandol for Louis, Duke of Anjou. Musée des Tapisseries at Angers, France.

was generally regarded as inert and resistant to any purposes, and where an original was considered superior to every imitation or repetition of the same thing. But it would be a mistake to suppose that early Christians believed all super-human spirits to be angels or devils. Like nearly all their contemporaries they saw the planets as signs from living creatures, whose powerful influence might be beneficent or hostile. The moon was also alive and changeable, as were other powers connected with the weather. Communication with these entities was dangerous, since any kind of politeness might be treated as idolatrous worship on both sides, but St Thomas Aquinas was probably not original in making an exception if the purpose was simply to obtain a weather forecast. St Antony of Egypt certainly thought that information obtained from demons in this respect might well be all right. However, in Christian myth it is generally true to say that such creatures as dragons tend to become demonic instead of chaotic, because this world in itself is regarded as a good thing.

Babylon and the Man of Sin

Most mythology in the New Testament is about the present and future reign of the kingdom of God among men. This orientation towards the future has parallels in Persia, but was against the grain of Greek civilisation and of the ancient world in general, where the golden age had been placed in the past. The speed of the Lord's second coming is exaggerated in terms of our time, but this pace is appropriate to myth, as in the days of the creation and in the lives of patriarchs before the flood. In cultures where mythology was taken for granted as a mode of seeing what cannot be otherwise expressed, the ex-travagance of the time scale would serve only to emphasise the enigmatic element in the story. Few, I believe, took the figures literally and did sums with them until the nature of mythical language had been forgotten or had at least receded to the background of consciousness.

In what are generally called the 'eschatological' passages in the New Testament – the prophecies of Christ in the Gospels and the visions of the future in the *Revelation of St John* – the end of the world is seen to be coming through the fall of Jerusalem to the Roman armies, and through the delayed, but inevitable, collapse of the Roman empire itself. No one was wrong who read Babylon in the *Revelation* as Rome when the empire was falling, or in the age of the Reformation when the same texts about a harlot on seven hills were applied to Papal Rome in the secular glories of the Italian Renaissance.

Because Rome is called Babylon, she can be much more. She is the world organised for power. But the details of her fall, in so far as they do relate to particular historical events, concern the working out of the situation confronting the seer, probably near the end of the first war of the legions in 68–70. He antici-pated another clash between military claimants to the imperial throne, and he was right, although this did not come until 193 and again in the troubles of the third century. He also expected further trouble in the east, where in the same troubled future the Roman Emperor fell into the hands of the Shah of Persia, the armies of Odenathus of Palmyra occupied Syria and Egypt,

and the streets of Alexandria ran red with blood in civil strife. The detailed imagery of the prophecy relates to the actual situation of the time, seen as always in a foreshortened scale.

The dragon and the various beasts are a special case. In one sense these images, like Babylon itself, are already anachronistic, echoes from a distant past when God was believed to have torn Rahab in pieces and made the world with them, as Marduk made it from the body of his adversary Tiamat in the Babylonian myth. But in another sense the 'mark of the beast' can stand for the animal in us, the aspect of sin that appears to us as a survival from an earlier stage of evolution. It may even be said that our own evolutionary myth represents a return to sources, and a reversal of the general trend of mythological development in the Church, where the dragon has become Satanic but intelligent, and the beast has become anti-Christ.

The myth of the false Messiah, the man of sin, has roots in the apocalyptic literature of Judaism between the two Testaments, before the foundation of the Christian Church. But in its Christian form it is perhaps best represented by an influential sermon ascribed to St Ephrem, who died about 373. This probably does belong to his time, though it certainly contains much earlier elements. Perhaps for this reason some hesitate to attribute it to an original poet of great distinction. What is most interesting is his description of the attractiveness of anti-Christ, who would not be an incarnation of Satan but his organ, exquisitely formed in the womb of a young girl whose morals would be distinctly loose. Her child would be not only beautiful, but apparently modest and humble, a determined fighter for social justice and an enemy of idolatry. He would grow up handsome, kind, courageous, and affable to all men, especially Jews, who would be among his firmest friends. He would put on a show of great modesty about his extraordinary performance in a number of fields, refusing gifts or other rewards for his good works, and so deceive everyone that all would unite to make him their king. But as soon as he had defeated some formidable opposition on the field of battle he would change his tune and reveal a sadistic side. While he would not cease from demonstrations of magical powers these would be illusions, for the mountains that disappeared would still be there and new islands in the sea would be no more than mirages. By these demonstrations he would obtain a great deal of enthusiastic applause, but it would then be discovered that

only his partisans, sealed with his mark on their forehead and right hand, would be able to survive, for the earth would have been devastated by the means used to subdue his foes. His power would last for three years and a half before the end of the world and the coming of Christ.

St Ephrem's sermon had much influence in eastern Christendom, especially in Russia. It lies behind a book by the religious philosopher Vladimir Soloviev, called in the English translation *War, Progress, and the End of History*. This was written in or before 1899. It may be said that Soloviev correctly anticipated the outcome of the Russo-Japanese war and the fall of the Russian empire, but he expected the Japanese to take over China and conquer Russia instead of south-east Asia, and then the west. He also foresaw their eventual defeat and the formation of a United States of Europe, more or less democratic, no longer materialistic, but profoundly uncertain of the validity of its Christian roots, with churches reduced in numbers but more conscious of their common Christianity. In these circumstances a man of genius comes to the fore who is elected President for life of the United States of Europe, and at a later stage Emperor of the entire world. He has begun as an authority on artillery, a man of business on a considerable scale, probably dealing in ornaments. 'His mother, a lady of doubtful reputation, was very well known in both hemispheres . . . The number of people who had grounds for considering him as their son was rather too great'. Early in life he compares himself to Christ, regarding himself as His true successor, but in a spiritual crisis he has a vision of a different kind of supreme being, who does not require his obedience but gives him his power as his own son. In the light of this he is able to write a book offering solutions to the world's most pressing problems. Universal satisfaction is given to the hungry, and displays based on a thorough investigation of all

Left:
The battle with the dragon of chaos as seen on a mirror handle from Enkomi in Cyprus, possibly made in Syria in the ninth century B.C. British Museum.
Far left:
The Christ child trampling on the dragon, who is also struck in the mouth by another heavenly figure, possibly the archangel Michael. Detail from a baldachin originally at one of the wooden stave-churches at Sagon in Norway. Historical Museum, Bergen.
Right:
Revelation 16, vv. 12–14. The seer is observing the whole from the left. The sixth angel blows his trumpet, while he or another releases four (not three as in v. 13) unclean spirits who are to collect the kings of the earth for the battle of the great day. The voice from under the altar speaks in French the substance of verse 12. From an MS of the thirteenth century. Trinity College Library, Cambridge.

48

A Greek icon of the fifteenth century showing John the Baptist praying in the wilderness protected by the hand of God. The scroll in his hand contains a passage from Matthew III. 2: 'Repent ye, for the kingdom of Heaven is at hand.'

the possibilities of oriental mysticism and magic are presented to the world's public with the aid of every kind of Anglo-American technical device. A temple for the unification of all cults is erected over the Dome of the Rock at Jerusalem, and in this he assembles a World Congress of Religions at which he presents a plan for the unification of all Christian churches. One condition is that they all recognise him as their protector and patron, but in his speeches on the subject he makes no reference to Christ. Many of the church leaders present are lured by the prospect of renewed political patronage, but the opposition is led by Pope Peter II, elected in Damascus on the way to the Congress, by a retired Russian bishop with a reputation as a staretz or spiritual director, generally known as 'the Elder John', and by 'the most learned German theologian, Professor Ernst Pauli'.

The 'elder' is a recognisable Russian type and the pope may be said to represent the papacy at its best, but in 1899 it required some prophetic gifts to envisage Professor Pauli. It is not so much a matter of his appearance and his mannerisms, but of what those mannerisms are meant to suggest that makes us see in him a figure like Karl Barth. The parallel between them is never more impressive than at the moment when he stands up, deserted by more than half of his theological colleagues, 'as if without a definite object in view', but then leads his small group across the empty seats to sit beside the pope and the remnant of the Orthodox. Soloviev's story is inevitably unfinished. What is more than personal about it is the vision of a final crisis between the Christian Church and the world organised for power, in which the churches in their worldly aspects will go over to the enemy but the men of faith will remain together. It is not the exchange of ideas that is open to objection but the use of religion for promoting a secular solidarity. A world congress of faiths assembled for this purpose might split on lines that would bring Christians and Buddhists, as well as Catholics and Protestants, together in opposition, and this is perhaps a political probability.

The New Jerusalem

The new heaven and earth in the last chapters of the New Testament, *Revelation* 21 and 22, are a Utopia with a difference. This is no place for cowards, for the doubleminded, for the cruel and lustful, or for those who deceive themselves and others by propaganda or other means. It is a city, a community, where mutual understanding is complete and all thirst is quenched by the water of life, all hunger by a tree with fresh fruit in every month. The foundations of the walls are precious stones, and also apostles, since this is a Christian vision, but they could be other founders of churches, communities, cultures. The gates are angels, pearls, and tribes of Israel, but they could be nations and eras in history.

This paradise or park is a city and a garden, in a new world, without a sea or sun, without night or day, church or temple, for its life is in the light of the Lamb of God. But this is not an allegory of some purely spiritual existence, but of the resurrection of the body. St Irenaeus reported, on the authority of those who had known the seer of the *Revelation,* that in the coming time the production of wine would immensely increase. In every vineyard ten thousand vines would carry ten clusters, with grapes in proportion. Every grape when pressed would yield twenty-five measures of wine, and every grain of corn ten pounds of clear clean flour. All the animals would be tame and live at peace with one another, with plenty of fodder. This vision of the future is no doubt related to the prophecy in *Isaiah* 11 that the wolf will lie down with the lamb, the lion will be a vegetarian, and very small children will put their hands into an adder's den without being bitten. But it is interesting to reflect that at the time of St Irenaeus the south of France was becoming a country of vineyards under the civilising influence of Rome. He was looking forward to more of them with sufficient corn and wine for rich and poor alike, for he was not expecting the ruin of Greek civilisation but the transformation of the Roman empire into the commonwealth of Christ. His time scale may have been wrong, as it always is in prophetic prediction, but he saw a vision hidden from the prophets of doom, of churches and vineyards near his home.

50

The *omphalos,* the navel of the earth on the
floor of the Catholicon in the Holy Sepulchre.
The present form of this is at least as old as the
Catholicon itself, which dates from the middle
of the eleventh century, but it could be very
much earlier if it is to be conceived as originally, like the rock of Golgotha itself, a preserved
part of the ground's surface, when other parts
were levelled for the building. The floor of the
Catholicon was redecorated by the Crusaders in
1142, and they may be responsible for some of
the ornament, but the sunflower shape that
concealed this until lately was the work of a
Greek in the nineteenth century.

Below left:

This picture may give some idea of the appearance of Golgotha at the end of the fourth
century, flanked by the circular Anastasis
around the Holy Sepulchre on the left, and on
the right by the Church of the Martyrion,
corresponding to the present chapel of St
Helena. This mosaic, which includes the
symbols of the evangelists above and Christ
teaching his apostles below, has no doubt
suffered much from repair, but retains a basis
from before 400. It is in the apse of St Puden-
ziana, Rome.

Below right:

A sixteenth-century engraving of Cuzco, the
Inca capital and, according to Inca tradition,
the navel of the earth.

The place of the skull

The centre of the earth

In many medieval representations of the crucifixion, a skull is under Christ's cross. All four Gospels say that Christ was crucified in a place called 'Golgotha, the place of the skull'. This could be so called because of the shape of the rock, as General Gordon supposed. It is much more likely that the name reflects the legend that Adam was buried in or near the centre of the earth, where he first was formed, and that this is somewhere in Palestine. The idea of the centre of the earth at a sacred mountain, in a place where heaven and earth meet, is common to a number of religions. It is found for instance among the Semangs of the Malay peninsula, who can show us the rock, Batu-Ribn, rising at the earth's centre. There, we are told, a tree used to grow right up into the sky. And at Apollo's temple at Delphi we can still see the *omphalos*, 'the navel of the earth', represented on the floor, 'the everlasting centre-stone of deeply murmuring earth', as Pindar put it in the sixth of his Pythian odes. The *omphalos* is also represented on the floor of the Catholicon in the Church of the Holy Sepulchre at Jerusalem, where a clear representation of the human navel, carved in the twelfth century, was concealed in the nineteenth in the interests of decency, but has lately been revealed again. In Palestine there were other world-centres. Shechem, for

52

instance, is called 'the navel of the land' in the *Book of Judges*
(9.37). But when Jerusalem is identified as 'the navel of the
earth', we may be reasonably sure that the original reference
is to the 'foundation rock', the *Eben Shetiyah* or *Es Sakra*,
which can still be seen under the Dome of the Rock in the
Temple area. This juts out over a large cavity where Abraham,
David and others are said to have prayed in particular places.

Jewish tradition affirms that the rock was within the Holy of
Holies in Solomon's Temple. Louis Ginzberg, in *Legends of
the Jews,* quotes a passage in the *Mishna* (Yoma 5.2): 'After
the Ark was taken away a stone remained there from the time
of the former prophets, and it was called Shetiyah. It was
higher than the ground by three finger-breadths.' The word
used for stone could be read as meaning a firestone, a thunder-
bolt. He himself supposed that a meteorite made the cavity
under the rock, and left the rock itself when 'the Lord
answered from heaven by fire' upon the threshing floor of
Araunah the Jebusite, and so sanctified this as the proper
place of sacrifice (*II Samuel* 24.16, *I Chronicles* 21.26), while
the Tabernacle made in the wilderness was still standing.
Ginzberg's concern was to establish a historical ground in the
Biblical account of David and Solomon for the sanctity of the
rock. Other scholars have pointed out a resemblance between it
and other natural altars known to have been used in the worship of the sun, and indeed between the general plan of Solomon's temple and sun-temples elsewhere in the Middle East.
They have often assumed that a hole in the bottom of the
cavity was intended to serve as a drain for an altar of burnt
offering, but closer investigation has shown that it has no
outlet. We may fairly suppose that the rock was an altar at one
time, but most probably before the Jewish occupation of
Jerusalem.

According to Jewish tradition, as we have seen, the rock was
concealed within the Holy of Holies. It was found while the
foundations of the Temple were being dug. David tried to
shift it, but the waters beneath rose and would have covered
the earth with another flood had not his counsellor Ahitophel
inscribed the name of God on the rock and let it fall. In a
version of this story the rock speaks and tells how God's
voice from Sinai made the whole world shake, and the rock
alone prevented its total dissolution, for it is the foundation
stone of all creation, the stone that God threw into the abyss
to divide the waters from the waters, and so indeed is 'the
navel of the earth'.

The Bible itself contains in *Genesis* 14 traces of a foundation
legend for the Temple at Jerusalem long before David and
Solomon in the account of Melchizedek, king of Salem and
priest of God the Most High, who received offerings from
Abraham and blessed him. The Samaritans identified Salem
with Schechem, but Jerusalem was almost certainly intended
by the compiler who incorporated this story into our book of
Genesis. The Samaritans also identified Melchizedek with
Shem, the son of Noah and the ancestor of all the Semitic
races. Shem, which means 'name', may well have been at one
time another name for the primal man, Adam.

The meeting of Abraham and Melchizedek,
with Christ looking down in blessing. Melchizedek brings out a basket of bread and a
large amphora of wine. Mosaic of the fourth
century at Sta Maria Maggiore, Rome.
Below:
The sacrifices of Abel (on the left), Melchizedek (in the centre) and Abraham (on the
right) in a very fine mosaic of the sixth century
at St Apollinare in Classe, near Ravenna.
Below left:
The ruins of the temple of Apollo at Delphi –
the navel of the earth in Greek tradition.

Epiphanius, a Christian expert on the history of heresies
who lived and wrote in the second half of the fourth century,
came from Palestine and was bishop for many years of Salamis
in Cyprus. Drawing on his considerable knowledge of local
traditions, he said that the Sidonians (Phoenicians) claimed
that Melchizedek was of Canaanite origin, the son of Astarte
and Heracles (the Greek name here conceals some local culture-hero), but the Jews said that he was the son of a prostitute
(doubtless of a temple-priestess at some Syrian shrine of
Astarte). Though later Jewish legends make him the
first builder of Jerusalem 'on the grave of our father
Adam', I think we may fairly assume that one line in Jewish
tradition, perhaps especially strong in Palestine where it was
known to Epiphanius, sought to depreciate the Gentile past of
Jerusalem before David, and more especially to insist on the
exclusively Israelite character of the foundation rock that still
marked the site of the Holy of Holies. If this tradition goes

back before the fall of Jerusalem, and before the time of the
New Testament, as is not unlikely, it may account for the use
of the name Golgotha, the place of the skull, for somewhere
outside the city.

A parallel may be seen on Mount Gerizim, where the
Samaritans will show to their friends their own original holy
place at some distance from their present place of sacrifice, but
at a like distance from the ruins of a Christian church erected
by the Emperor Justinian on the site of the Samaritan Temple.
In this case it seems most probable that Justinian did build on
the original site. The Samaritans made the best of it, but were
later driven even farther from the spot. So the navel of the
earth may have moved from the *Eben Shetiyah* in the Holy of
Holies to Golgotha outside the walls.

A number of passages in the Talmud allow that the centre
of the world is in Palestine, as is indeed plausible even today in
relation to the old world of Europe, Asia and Africa. Some
name Jerusalem without referring to the rock. The tomb of
Adam is sometimes located with that of Abraham at Hebron,
but this may be to keep it out of Jerusalem. It is not at all
unlikely that the name Golgotha points to a belief that Adam's
skull was there, perhaps with other skulls thrown outside the
walls when the Temple was built, rebuilt or restored. In so far
as this was a myth of the centre, of the origin of the world and
of human life in or near Golgotha, it would have a Gentile,
anti-Jewish character, and this may account for the erection
of a temple of Aphrodite, the Canaanite Ashtaroth or Astarte,
on or near the spot in Hadrian's time.

The discovery of the crosses near the Holy
Sepulchre and the miraculous verification of the
cross of Christ by a healing miracle as represented by Piero della Francesca in a series of
frescoes made by him about 1551. Church of
St Francis at Arezzo, Italy.

Built on the site of Herod's temple in Jerusalem,
this Muslim shrine contains the rock which was
believed to be the centre of the earth.
Hence 'The Dome of the Rock'.

The sacrifice of Isaac

Some connection between Jewish and Gentile worship at Jerusalem is implied in the identification of the hill of Sion with 'the mount of the Lord' in 'the land of Moriah' where Abraham offered his child of promise, born to him in his old age, in sacrifice to his God. This part of the story of Abraham has made a deep impression on all his spiritual descendants, Jews, Christians and Moslems, but they have not found it easy to agree about the significance of the *Akedah*, the sacrifice of Isaac. It is generally taken as marking the decisive point of divergence between Israel and the surrounding nations, in that Israel rejected the form of sacrifice that is described in the Old Testament as 'passing children through the fire to Moloch'. Most modern scholars agree that in this context 'Moloch' is the name not of a god but of a particular kind of sacrifice. This is generally considered to be the sacrifice of a life, of a lamb or of a child, to the powers of death and darkness in order to avert disaster to the community at large.

However, it is not easy to interpret the story of the sacrifice of Isaac in terms of a downright condemnation of this or any other kind of human sacrifice, since the command to offer him up is clearly given by the Lord God himself, and his father's obedience is commended. Moreover, it is clear that according to one strand of Jewish tradition Isaac *was* sacrificed, but returned from the dead. He was a willing sacrifice, and as his father loosed his bonds he himself spoke the benediction: 'Blessed be the Lord, who quickens the dead.' According to a story in the same line of tradition he was carried to heaven by the angels and lived there for three years. When Abraham came back without him his mother died of shock, or in another variant, from the violence of her joy in the discovery that after all he was still alive. This points to the possiblity that the sacrifice of the first-born need not mean his destruction, but rather his solemn initiation in a mode that God would command and provide, including a sacrifice for him. According to the expanded version of the story given by Ginzberg, Abraham at first doubted his priestly power to sacrifice, and asked whether 'the high priest Shem' should do it. He told Sarah that he was taking Isaac to Shem and his son Eber, that he might learn the Lord's ways. This version seems to be a reference to the Shem-Melchizedek story.

All initiations into new life are dangerous, and many involve a real risk of death. Some such initiations no doubt provide a ritual outlet for the jealousy which the older men may feel for the new initiates but the symbolical purpose, for instance of circumcision (whatever hygienic uses it may or may not have), is not to kill or castrate the baby, but to bring new strength in a form that signifies dedication to a role, male or female, as ritual drowning in Christian baptism means death and resurrection in Christ. In the case of circumcision what was an initiation to adolescence came to be given to infants, not out of sadism, but because they are passive in the hands of the ministers, and therefore less likely to be seriously hurt than small boys. Yet even in infancy accidents do happen, and the death of the baby may be regarded as one way of acceptance of

Alo eñ weteñ finiet al openbaer
Wele dattet cruys ons heuy waer
Soe namen fi die twee crucen daer
Ende fi legdenfe op eneñ doden dat is waer

Hier gheeft hem die engbel drye graynen claer
Die fal hi begrauen met finen vader
Daer of fal waffen eneñ boeme goet
Daer xpriftus aen fal ftoruen fijn bloet

a ij

Hier comt die engbel wilt my verftaen
Tot deñ coninck dauid ghegaen
Ende hi heeft hem binneñ dyen dagheñ
Die roeden tot ifuerufalem deñ draggbeñ

the sacrifice by the god. A number of infants whose skeletons
have been found buried in places associated with sacrificial
victims may have died in the course of such rites or may even
have died a natural death (in our terms, for in many cultures
no death is natural). But the complete identification of the
acceptance of the sacrifice with the destruction of the victim is
a sign of religious perversion in pagan and Christian religion.

It is not at all surprising that the evidence for ritual infanticide should be a good deal more abundant in Phoenician
Africa, especially in the Roman period, than in Syria and
Palestine, where the historical references to the sacrifice
of children refer to extreme emergencies, after other sacrifices
may be presumed to have failed. In times of crisis, when the
crops are ruined by storms, when the city is besieged, and
when sons rebel against their fathers, an appeal may be made
to a primitive custom of sacrificing the first-born, on the ground
that the first baby is 'redeemed with a lamb'. But this is not a
historical explanation of the origins of animal sacrifice, any
more than most descriptions of primitive Christianity are based
on real evidence about its origins. In Carthage, as in Mexico
and in some parts of the South Seas, human sacrifice, especially of prisoners and of infants, does seem to have become a
normal part of religious devotion to destruction, but this is a
perversion of paganism, which begins in devotion to powers of
growth which are also destructive, because the death of one
year is an indispensable condition for the growth of another.
A like perversion of Christian religion can lead to the total
identification of the sacrifice of Christ with his death on the
cross, and of self sacrifice with the destruction or mutilation of
all the powers of our natural life. This is not to deny the
presence in us of fear of life, and fear of the next generation,
but the 'battered baby syndrome' is not the foundation of any
religion. It is a heresy or deviation to which educators of the
young are especially liable.

Melchizedek

But we are here concerned with Christian not pagan mythology. In Christian history Golgotha is the place of the crucifixion and resurrection of Jesus Christ – 'In the place where he

Six illustrations from a Dutch book called
Historia Sanctae Crucis or *Boec van den Houte*,
printed at Kuilenburg in 1483 by John Veld-
ener. They are taken from one of the very few
surviving copies, the one in the Royal Library
at Brussels. (a) The miraculous testing of the
true cross. (b) The Archangel Michael gives to
Seth three seeds from the tree of life. These
he will plant under Adam's tongue when he
buries him. (c) King David is told in a dream
to bring the rod of Moses to Jerusalem. (d)
King David uses the rod or rods to heal the
sick. (e) The beam rejected by the builders
becomes a bridge. (f) The Queen of Sheba
refuses to cross it.

Hier trect dauid die roeden goet
Oder aerden des hijt wel vroet
Ende hi heefter die sielen mede gheraect
Alse de si sijn van allen siecten ghesont ghemaect

Hier sullen die ioden sul di verstaen
Die se ut ouer een ryuier ghedaen
Claerlijcken soe seldije verstaen
Om dat men daer ouer soude gaen

b iij

Hier coemt als wy verstaen
Die coninegghinne van saba ghegaen
Ende si maecte hoer baruoet
Genieuen den houte dat si ouerwoet

was crucified was a garden, and in the garden a new tomb'—but in Christian myth it is also the grave of Adam and the shrine of Melchizedek. In Psalm 110, one of the enthronement psalms, which was probably used at the coronation of the kings of Judah, perhaps at an annual feast where they were enthroned again, the opening verse runs;

The Lord says to my lord
Sit at my right hand,

Later the psalm continues: 'The Lord has sworn and will not change his mind, "You are a priest for ever after the order of Melchizedek."' This psalm is quoted several times in the New Testament by Christ himself in the synoptic Gospels, and of Christ in the *Acts* and Epistles. The verse about Melchizedek dominates the central part of the *Epistle to the Hebrews*. The author of the Epistle was right in seeing in this verse some sense of contrast between the Levitical priesthood and the royal priesthood of the house of David. The king is a superior priest, not only because of his royalty, but because in representing Melchizedek, king and priest of Jerusalem, he represents primal man, 'without father, without mother, without genealogy'.

It is not an accident, the author of *Hebrews* thinks, that Melchizedek has no place in the genealogies of *Genesis*. He could not have one if he was Shem, and a figure of Adam. Later Christians, elaborating the idea of Melchizedek as a figure of Christ, to whom Abraham and his seed paid tithes on the site of Jerusalem, identified him with the angel of the Lord, and so with the Holy Spirit. The group called Melchizedekians, who penetrated to Rome at the end of the second century, thought of him as the Word and Spirit of God, the Second Person of the Trinity, who came to rest on Jesus Christ and made him the Third. Some traces of their ideas appear in later legend, in the angel who shows the way to Shem and Melchizedek, as they carry the body or the head of Adam from the hold of Noah's Ark to the centre of the earth, as well as in some features of Melchizedek's appearance and dress. But in the interests of orthodoxy he has been provided with a pedigree, despite the *Epistle to the Hebrews*.

In one version of the story he is an antediluvian baby, born

58

mysteriously to an aged mother, the wife of Nir, Noah's
brother. After her death he was found sitting by her and wip-
ing his clothes like a child of three years old, 'glorious in
countenance' and 'having the seal of the priesthood on his
breast'. He blessed the Lord with his lips, and ate the blessed
bread without any delay. But in another version of the story he
is a grandson or great-grandson of Shem, who nevertheless
survives to take him on the long journey from the Ark to
Jerusalem. His father and mother are Malakh and Yozadak.
Malakh is called the son of Cainan, who in another version is
Melchizedek's father and is carefully distinguished from
Canaan the son of Ham, who was cursed by Noah. Nevertheless the pedigree represents an attempt to reconcile Canaanite
and Semitic tradition in regard to one who was a culture-hero
for both peoples.

The story properly begins with Noah and his sons carrying
the body of Adam from his first grave in 'the cave of treasures'
(with the other patriarchs before the flood) into the Ark. Shem,
Ham and Japhet brought gold, incense and myrrh. But Shem
alone took the body out again, following Noah's instructions.
He then sealed the Ark with his father's seal so that no one
else could get in, or discover what he had done, and set out
secretly on a tour of exploration with Melchizedek, leaving the
rest of his family in the charge of his two brothers. The angel
of the Lord met them and made their way swift and easy to
the centre of the earth. There 'the four corners separated from
each other, and the earth opened in the form of a cross'. Shem
and Melchizedek let down the body of Adam, whereupon 'the
four quarters drew quickly together, and the door of the
created world was shut fast'. The place was called by four
names, Karkaphtha, the skull, Gaghulta, 'because it was round',
Resiphta, 'down-trodden, because the head of . . . Satan was
crushed there', and Gefifta, 'because all the nations were to be
gathered to it'.

On the following morning Melchizedek built an altar of
twelve stones and offered bread and wine, which Shem had
brought from the garden of Eden. According to Noah's directions he stayed there as priest of the shrine. He was not allowed
to build a house or to offer any animal sacrifice, or any oblation
but bread and wine. He wore a lion's skin and lived as a hermit, cutting neither his hair nor his nails. His image is like
Eastern ikons of St John the Baptist, who is often provided
with wings, for he too, like Elijah, is a figure of the angelic life.
Shem told his family that he was dead, and buried where he
died. This may be a way of identifying his grave with Adam's
own, but in this story he lived to welcome Abraham and to
have Jerusalem built for him by twelve kings, including those
who figure in *Genesis* 14 as allies of Abraham.

These stories appear in *The Book of the Cave of Treasures*,
a Syrian compilation which in its present form can hardly be
earlier than the sixth century, though much of its material
may have been put together in the fourth. The stories are
closely associated with a chronological framework of years of
the world, which sets the incarnation in the middle of the
sixth millenium from the beginning. The seventh thousand

The Ruthwell Cross on which some lines from
The Dream of the Rood are written. The date of
the cross is still in dispute, but it could be
nearly as old as the poem, and is almost certainly earlier than the Danish invasions of the
ninth and tenth centuries. The risen Lord is
about to ascend to the Father in the central
panel. The church that now surrounds the cross
is the Parish church of Ruthwell, near
Dumfries in the lowlands of Scotland.

The world tree represented in a carving at Urnes stave church in Norway. In Scandinavian tradition the fabric of the universe was maintained by a gigantic ash tree which always remained green.

years, the sabbath of the Lord's reign, was on this calculation due to begin about 500 A.D. Julius Africanus, to whom the calculation is attributed, lived in the middle of the third century. Despite his name, he was a citizen of Emmaus in Palestine, and a friend of a princely family in Osrhoene in northern Syria. He is certainly cited as saying that Adam was buried in Golgotha, and I think he may be responsible for recording a great deal more. His free use of Gentile sources, especially in the Syriac-speaking area, to supplement the Old Testament, enabled him to take a liberally long view of the age of the earth. The stories in *The Book of the Cave of Treasures* are also found in a rather different form in the *Annals* of Eutychius, Patriarch of Alexandria in the middle of the tenth century, a Syrian physician whose Arabic name was Said Ibn Batrik. I think the common source must be a collection written while the chronological framework invented by Julius Africanus was more than a convention. The collection very likely included more of his own work than can now be identified by explicit quotations elsewhere.

The legend of the Cross

None of these books, however, make any connection between the cross of Christ and the trees in the garden of Eden. This is a later development that arose partly from a growing interest in the relics of the true cross, and partly from the conversion of peoples accustomed to holy trees. It is important to notice that there is no reference to any remains of the true cross in the earliest accounts of discoveries made on Golgotha by the Emperor Constantine's mother, the Dowager-Empress Helena, in or soon after 326. The earliest reference to them, in a sermon by St Cyril of Jerusalem around the middle of the fourth century, speaks already of fragments scattered all over the world. Not until the end of the century are we told the story of three separate crosses found in or near the Holy Sepulchre, with Pilate's original inscription, 'Jesus of Nazareth, the King of the Jews'. This, we are told, was loose, and did not help to distinguish the cross of Christ from those of the two thieves; for that a miracle was needed.

By this time the discovery of the cross is closely connected with Helena's other discoveries, but there is a Syrian version in which the finder is not Helena, but a princess of Osrhoene or Edessa, working in association with a bishop of Jerusalem, Cyriacus, whose name appears fifth in the early lists. Although the details are clearly borrowed from later stories where the royal finder is able to give orders to the local authorities with the certainty of imperial power behind her, I think the story may point to some concern with the remains of the cross at a time when they could exist, perhaps while the foundations of Aphrodite's temple were being dug. That this temple was built over a cemetery is an ascertained fact, for two unfinished tombs can be seen under the level of Constantine's foundations, which were certainly set on the temple's site after a good deal of earth had been cleared away. We may therefore be reasonably certain that the church of the Holy Sepulchre is outside the walls of the original old city demolished by Hadrian, nor is it hard to imagine the marks of identification that might be borne by Christ's empty tomb, when we consider the temptations of devout visitors in all centuries, including the first. So far we are on historical ground. The earliest accounts of Helena's work refer to the Martyrium, the church that was built on Golgotha, the Anastasis, the Rotunda round the Holy Sepulchre, and the rock, or part of the rock left when the rest was levelled to carry a figure of the cross.

The traditional site of the 'invention', or discovery, of the cross itself is not the Holy Sepulchre, but a discarded cistern of the appropriate period, which was probably found and cleared while the Martyrium was being built. The fragments referred to by St Cyril may have been found there, or they may perhaps have been in circulation in places like Edessa before Helena's discoveries made relics of the passion popular. What is important is that all our earliest references are to fragments or to objects made with nails from the crucifixion. No one claims to have seen the whole cross, and it should be obvious that nothing found intact would have been broken so soon. The number of fragments of the true cross may be best explained if we assume that every bit of wood gathered near the site became a relic, and in many cases a means whereby a sense of direct contact with Christ was communicated. Miraculous healings were the result of faith, not of the application of a particular holy object, but it is not surprising that they should be taken as evidence of the authenticity of the relics.

What may be called the prehistory of the cross became interesting as the crucifix became a central religious symbol. The simplest and most widely diffused form of the legend of its origin survives in the name 'Adam's apple' for the epiglottis. This is based on a just-so story of how man got his apple, that the fruit of the knowledge of good and evil got stuck in Adam's throat. From the seed, after he was buried, one or three trees grew, of which one was the crucifix. In more elaborate versions of the same myth these seeds are planted in his throat after his death by his son Seth. They belong to the tree of life, not to the tree of knowledge of good and evil, and they have been brought from Eden with the oil of mercy to console the last hours of Adam. A sapling from this root became the staff or the rod of Moses. King David found it, used it for various wonders, and planted it in his garden. Cut down for Solomon's temple, it would not fit into the building. Rejected and flung into a ditch, it rose to the surface and became a bridge. The Queen of Sheba was about to cross it when she recognised its nature and destiny, and took off her shoes to ford the stream below. By her advice Solomon put it in the Temple after all, as a lintel over a door, overlaid with gold and silver. But his wicked grandson Abijah stripped off the precious metals and buried it on the spot where the pool of Bethesda was afterwards dug. There the virtue of the wood, as well as the ministry of the angel, gave power to the waters to cure all who were afflicted, until as the time of the passion drew near the beam came to float on the surface, from whence it was taken to become the wood of the cross.

Elsewhere there are traces of another folktale in which the tree for the crucifixion comes directly from the courts of the

The fifth century ivory called The Holy Women at the Sepulchre, from the Trivulzio Collection in Milan. In the upper register the guards can be seen, sleeping. In the lower the women arrive at the sepulchre on Easter morning.

The triumph of the cross, restored to Jerusalem by the Emperor Heraclius after his victory over the Persians in 629, as represented by Piero della Francesca in the frescoes made by him at Arezzo around 1451.

Temple, where it may have been supposed to grow in or near the original Golgotha, the *Shetiyah*. In another version it is Eve who takes out of Eden the fatal branch of the tree of knowledge, and plants it where from white it turns to green with the birth of her children, and then to red at Abel's death. King Solomon's queen made 'spindles' from wood of the three colours still to be found in this tree (or trees?) and put them up to carry the curtains of the royal bed, perhaps for magical reasons related to birth and death. There they were found in Solomon's ship by the knights engaged in the quest for the Holy Grail. This particular story is first found in texts of the first quarter of the thirteenth century, but the materials must be much older and need not necessarily be connected with the wood of the cross, for Eve here could be 'the mother of all living', a goddess of birth and death, of creation and destruction, whose woods had magical properties, and Solomon's ship may have belonged to another wise king.

Neither the *Vexilla Regis* of Venantius Fortunatus nor *The Dream of the Rood* can properly be classed as mythology, but both show how such mythology could grow, for in *The Dream*, which was probably written in Northumbria towards the end of the seventh century, the cross narrates the story of the passion from its own point of view, telling how 'I was hewn down at the wood's end', as well as how 'I saw the mankind's lord swiftly come with courage, for he willed to mount

63

In this stained-glass window the skull of Adam and other human bones at the foot of the cross are particularly plain, as are the angels collecting the precious blood from the hands, feet and side of Christ. Angers Cathedral.

on me'. So Venantius, a Frank of the sixth century, appealed to the cross to bend:

> For awhile the ancient rigour
> That thy birth bestowed, suspend,
> And the king of heavenly beauty
> On thy bosom gently tend.

Both poets came from a culture that had worshipped gods who lived in and on the branches of a great tree, and a great god, Odin, who had hung from a tree, a sacrifice to himself. In this northern mythology the tree is greater and older than any particular god, itself perhaps a goddess in the first place, and this colours the centrality of the crucifixion in the Western medieval and then in the Protestant presentation of the work of Christ. But the root of the connection between the tree of life and Christ's death on the cross goes back to the beginnings of Christianity. Jesus, the second Adam, dying on Golgotha, the place of Adam's skull, must pass down the tree into the nether world, to the root of the tree in his throat, and come up again through the sepulchre, bringing Adam and Eve with him, for hell must be harrowed if the human race are to be saved. The fruit of the tree, of life or of knowledge, must be below the crucifix, on the way whereby Christ finds man, even at hell's bottom.

The harrowing of hell

The Evangelical symbols in the Book of Kells. The first leaf of this priceless Irish manuscript of the eighth century shows St Matthew, upper left, represented by the Man, to emphasize the human aspect of Christ. St Mark, the Lion, is seen on the upper right, symbolising the power and royal dignity. Lower left is St Luke, represented by the sacrificial calf. Lower right is the Eagle, representing St John, the evangelist who soars to heaven and gazes on the truth with clear unclouded eyes.

The *Descent into Hell* in what has come to be called the *Gospel of Nicodemus* is a folk tale rather than a work of art. It is made up of themes that had already taken literary form in earlier writings, more especially in parts of the Old and New Testaments, and it has itself grown from version to version in Greek and in translation. In its earliest forms it has come to be ascribed to two of the risen ones who, according to a passage the *Gospel of St Matthew* (27.52–53), were seen in and around Jerusalem at the time of Christ's resurrection. This is an afterthought, intended to raise the evidence for it to something like the level of witness to the appearances of the risen body of Christ, but the account is evidently older than the story in which it is set. It is important as the primary source of lore that took shape later in the mystery plays of the Middle Ages and in the *Vision of Piers Plowman*.

Descent into Hell

The tale begins at midnight in the nether world. There rose in the darkness something like the light of the sun. All rejoiced, especially Abraham, or in other versions Adam, saying: 'This shining comes from a great light'. Isaiah and John the Baptist began to repeat their prophecies, John adding a warning to idolaters to take their last chance to repent by worshipping Christ. A dialogue follows between Death and Satan, who warns Death against Jesus and his fraudulent claims. Death is frightened, for he has lost Lazarus, and now fears to lose all the dead. 'For I see that all whom I have swallowed up from the beginning of the world are disturbed. I have a pain in my stomach.' During this conversation thunder peals: 'Lift up your gates, rulers, and be lifted, everlasting doors, and the King of glory shall come in.' Satan and his demons try to bar the gates, crying: 'Who is this King of glory?' But the prophets mock them, especially Isaiah and King David, and the angels answer: 'The Lord mighty in battle.' The gates of brass break and the bars of iron yield and are crushed; the bound are set free, and all the dark places of death are lit up. Death and his company protest: 'Who is he who has so much power over the living and the dead?' But Christ in his turn seizes Satan by the head and hands him over to the angels, telling them to gag his mouth and bind him hand and foot. Then he gives him to Death, saying: 'Take him and hold him fast until my second coming.'

While Death pours scorn on Satan, Christ lifts up Adam and takes him to paradise with all the other patriarchs, prophets, martyrs and 'forefathers', blessing them all with the sign of the cross. Paradise here is in heaven and in Eden, for they meet Enoch and Elijah at the gate, but the penitent thief, who joined them as they were speaking to the translated patriarchs, has come in by the gate of the Flaming Sword that barred the way back into Eden in *Genesis* 3.24, where he gave Christ's promise as a password. In some sense the risen dead are certainly thought to be on earth, for some of them were baptized in the Jordan and kept the passover of the resurrection in Jerusalem.

Orpheus charming the beasts. Catacomb of Domitilla, Rome.
Right:
The Good Shepherd, mosaic of the fourth century in the Basilica Theodoriana, Aquileia, north Italy.
Below:
The Resurrection as seen by Piero della Francesca. The soldiers guarding the tomb lie sleeping while Christ ascends. From the fresco in the Palazzo Communale, Borgo San Sepolcro.

The absence of any clear distinction between this and the general resurrection seems to me to be a sign that the core of the story is early. The single reference to the second coming seems to be to an earlier form of the story of Satan's binding than appears in the *Revelation of St John* 20.2. Much of the material, as we have seen, consists in quotations from *Isaiah* and the *Psalms*. Moreover, the persons of the drama are already present in *I Corinthians*, which on any calculation is one of the earliest of St Paul's Epistles, themselves the earliest writings in the New Testament. In chapter 2, v. 8, we find 'the rulers of this age' who do not understand the hidden wisdom of God, which God decreed before the ages for our glorification'. If they had 'they would not have crucified the Lord of glory'. The reference is not primarily to the powers of church and state, to Caiaphas and Pilate, but to the cosmic principalities who are worsted in the harrowing of hell. In chapter 15 'For as by a man came death, by a man has come also the resurrection of the dead. For as in Adam all die, so also in Christ shall all be made alive . . . For he must reign until he has put all his enemies under his feet. The last enemy to be destroyed is death.' This is the language of myth, of the myth that is told consecutively, if rather badly, in *I Peter* 3.18–22, and by anticipation in words put into Christ's mouth in the *Gospel of St John* (5.25–9): 'The hour is coming and now is, when the dead will hear the voice of the Son of God, and those who hear will live'. This is the hour 'when all who are in the tombs will hear his voice and come out, those who have done good, to the resurrection of life, and those who have done evil, to the resurrection of judgement'. This is both the harrowing of hell and the general resurrection. Because Christ has been raised and has raised the dead, Christians are risen with Christ and will rise again at the resurrection. So long as mythology remained a familiar language this was not a problem. It was possible to combine expectations of the millenial reign of Christ, sometimes expressed in terms of luscious harvests of

very large bunches of grapes, with a sense of present participation in the risen life, not only through the eucharistic bread and cup, but in love of the brethren at feasts where some very exacting widows and virgins were commonly entertained.

The early Christians lived in a world inhabited, in the general view, by a multitude of demons and some angels. They believed that Christ and the angels had inflicted a decisive defeat on the demons, and that their final ruin was only a matter of time. Much of their continued influence was due to the illusions of those who believed them to be gods and goddesses. But Christians were careful to exorcise converts from paganism, lest 'a strange spirit' should remain with them. Those on the penumbra between Christian and pagan religion, which was fairly extensive in the second and third centuries, took a larger view of the powers of evil in the present world, which was fairly extensive in the second and third centuries. Such Gnostic groups as were looking for a way out to a higher sphere regarded Christ as a divine spirit who had come into this world from outside. He had never been born in the natural sense, but had manifested himself in a blaze of light that no human eye could bear. The light faded until the child materialised and went of his own accord to his mother. This Christ was a god or archangel, who had come to man's rescue like many another god, goddess or hero.

Figures of Christ

Christians who rejected this description found it difficult to present him as divine and human. For this and for other reasons, he is seldom directly portrayed in the art of catacombs, though he does sometimes appear as a child in the arms of his mother, or at his baptism in the Jordan. Most of the pictures in the Roman catacombs are signs of his presence and his work. There are quite a number of representations of Jonah swallowed and regurgitated by the whale, for 'as Jonah was in the whale's belly three days and three nights, so shall the Son of Man be in the heart of the earth'. Other favourites are Noah in the ark and Daniel in the den of lions. The raising of Lazarus is sometimes represented, and the parable of the good shepherd finding his lost sheep.

With these one scene from pagan myth is common, Orpheus with his lyre, generally charming the beasts. The depiction of Orpheus is often taken as an indication of Christian interest in poems and oracles ascribed to him, as if he were a kind of pagan prophet of the coming of Christ. But it is more likely that he stands for the long line of those who descend to the realms of the dead, Ishtar or Astaroth to rescue Baal, Heracles to find Persephone, and Orpheus to recover his lost Eurydice. Of all those heroes of mythology Orpheus is the most human, the most touching, and the most persuasive. He used charm rather than guile or force. And if he failed, for he looked back and saw his wife fading away behind him, this could be taken as a sign of universal human need for what only a man who was more than a man could do. Christianity in the second century was one of the mystery religions that offered participation in a common life to displaced persons, slaves and freedmen, widows and orphans, in the back streets of Hellenistic cities.

It differed from the other mysteries, including most of its own
heretical variants, in offering more than a passport to heaven
for initiates. There was a promise of transformation on this
earth, and an earnest of this in the common life of Christian
communities. At first it had very few followers in the educated classes. They were drawn towards it by the contempt of
the philosophers for pagan mythology.

I see no reason to suppose that the Christian myth was more
acceptable to the educated than other and older mythologies.
On the contrary the style of the narrative was barbarous and
crude, and the central episode of the crucifixion was monstrous. Nevertheless, by the third century an increasing number of men and women of some education were becoming
Christians, because of the attraction of some Christian ideas
and of the life of some Christian communities. As they came
to accept the myth as their own, their first inclination was to
turn it into a literary allegory. Alexandrian professors had
done this with Egyptian and Greek myths. Philo, as we have
seen, had read the Old Testament as allegory in the first
century A.D., and Origen applied the same methods to the
whole of the Christian scriptures in the first half of the third.

Allegory and deceit

These methods were widely used, but never completely
accepted or indiscriminately applied. The reaction against
some kinds of allegorising may be in the end more important
than any allegorical method, for it led to a general acceptance,
at least in theory, of the primacy of the literal or historical
sense. As we have seen in the introduction, this is not the
literal sense in our modern use of the term. No educated or
uneducated early Christian was what we should call a funda-
mentalist, but many of them did insist that the Bible is history,
as indeed most of it is, and not in the first place a fable concealing mystical truth or moral teaching. The allegorical
approach had important consequences in the emphasis that
came to be given to the possible symbolic significance of every
detail in the sacred stories. The tropological or moral approach,
which often went with it, called attention to problems about
the morality of myth that had long engaged philosophers.
Were the Christian stories any more edifying than some pagan
myths? Might the same objections be made to them?

Two matters in particular came to be matters of contention
and therefore of emphasis. The first was the question of guile.
Did Christ cheat? Was the whole story of his conflict with
Satan the tale of an ingenious deception whereby the demons
were made to believe that they had in their hands no more
than a perfectly innocent man, only to discover too late that he
was God in human form, and could not be held down?
Those who regarded the whole of Homer and much of the
Bible as a series of ingenious allegories concealing pearls of
wisdom too precious for vulgar eyes were not very much
shocked by the thought that Christ's human body and life
were so much bait to catch Satan on the concealed hook of his
godhead. Later generations were troubled, especially in those
classes where the rules of fair play are an important part of
professional military morals. It became essential to the argu-

A Russian icon with scenes from the life of
St Basil, who died in 379 at Caesarea in Cap-
padocia. The scenes at the top refer to his
birth, education and vocation, those on each
side to his episcopate and labours for the
church, those at his feet to his relationships
with his married brother, St Gregory of Nyssa,
and his sister, St Macrina, and to his death and
funeral. The icon is of the fourteenth century.
Hann Collection.

ment that the devil was the first to cheat, that he had beguiled Eve by concealing himself in an adder, as Christ beguiled him by concealing himself in a man.

Dialogue on this point takes up no little space in the mystery plays, but may best be illustrated from *Piers Plowman*. Here Lucifer claims that the Lord of heaven himself laid down that if Adam ate of the tree, all were to die and come and live with 'us devils'. Since this threat was made by Truth, and such a law by the Lord of light, he cannot claim the least of them back. But Satan, who is here distinguished from Lucifer or the devil, expresses his dread, for 'you got them by guile and broke into his garden'. Other demons complain that treason gives no true title against God. One in particular complains that God has been going about with a man's gait for thirty years. He has tried to tempt him, and has sometimes asked him awkward questions, but has never got (from his own point of view) satisfactory answers. He warned Pilate's wife in the hope that Christ's life might be lengthened, and the evil day postponed, but he now sees a soul coming with glory and great light. Lucifer's lying has lost the demons all their prey.

The theme of guile is taken up again in a triumphant speech by Christ himself. Good faith demands that grace should destroy guile, and as Adam and his kind died through a tree, it is right that through a tree they should return to life.

> And gile is bi-giled
> And in his gile fallen.

An element of deceit is involved in most, if not in all, myths of rescue from death. A sop must be thrown to Cerberus, Pluto's dog, or the music of Orpheus must charm him and other demons so that they do not bark. Even the goddess who descended to the realms of death in the Ras Shamra tablets had to take off her insignia, partly no doubt for the purpose of disguise.

All these tales are of robbery with violence. In the traditional account of the descent into hell Christ comes as a thief in the night. He is not disguised as a departing spirit, but accompanied by a superior force of angels, prepared to force the gates. Is this just? The question then arises of the ransom price to be paid, and of the devil's right of possession, legitimate or otherwise. This was the second question that troubled the Christian Fathers, and gave more trouble to the schoolmen of the Middle Ages.

Ransom and sacrifice

The debate revolved around the word 'ransom'. Christ himself was believed to have spoken of his life as 'a ransom for many'. At the time the reference certainly was to a way of liberating slaves. That the master was entitled to a price was acknowledged, but it is very unlikely that the early Christian community, consisting largely of slaves and freed slaves, would have considered that the payment of a price itself admitted a right of ownership, or would have felt any great scruples about the fair price for release. Many lived in the atmosphere of hard bargaining that is still characteristic of the back streets of Syrian towns. I do not think they would have found the idea that, from the devil's standpoint, Christ was under weight, repulsive or shocking. Something of this atmosphere lingers in the discussion of the subject by St Gregory of Nyssa towards the end of the fourth century.

'Those who have sold their own liberty for money are slaves of their purchasers ... It is not permissible for them or for any other person to claim liberty on their behalf ... While if someone through concern for the one so sold used violence against the purchaser, he would be regarded as wrong in trying to rescue by arbitrary means one who has been legally bought, there is no law to prevent him from buying the slave himself. So, as we had sold ourselves of our own will, it was necessary for him who sought our rescue ... to use no arbitrary method, but one consistent with justice. One such method was to put it in the power of our master (i.e. the devil) to receive what ransom he considered proper.'

Having laid down the conditions for a bargain, St Gregory reflects on the kind of price that Satan might accept. He considers Christ's birth, life and miracles from a diabolical standpoint, rather like C. S. Lewis in *The Screwtape Letters*, and concludes that the devil might very well think Jesus of Nazareth a very superior specimen of the human race, and far more useful for the exercise of power, his main concern, than a collection of lost souls in prison. He therefore accepted the bargain as he understood it, and had no right to complain that 'the Godhead was hidden under the cloak of our nature, that it might be within the grasp of the purchaser, and that as in the case of fish, the hook of the divinity might be swallowed under the bait of the flesh'.

But another St Gregory, of Nazianzus, the friend and contemporary of St Gregory of Nyssa and his brother St Basil, could not accept the traditional notion that a ransom was paid to the devil. He did not object to the deception of Satan, but he insisted that any ransom paid must be one and the same as Christ's sacrifice to the Father. At the same time he rejects any literal reading of the 'ransom' metaphor. 'If the Father accepts the blood of his Son, it is not because he asked for it or had need of it, but by reason of the economy of salvation, that men might be sanctified through the taking of manhood into God.' The purpose of God was to deliver us himself, 'having triumphed over the tyrant by force', and to bring us back to himself through his Son's redeeming action.

This reading of 'ransom' is neither traditional nor literal. It is clearly conditioned by the idea that the sacrifice of Christ is the hallowing of the perfect priest and victim in the incarnation of Christ, perfect God and perfect man, to do the will of God and to pour out his life in blood on the cross in Golgotha, and, if the metaphor be extended, to rise again and present himself at the heavenly altar. This is metaphor rather than myth, an interpretation of Christ's person, of his life, death and resurrection, in terms of traditional ritual. The Greek Christian writers are inclined to take for granted the idea that a perfectly satisfactory victim should perfectly represent the god to whom it is offered as well as the men who offer it. If this is so, to present Christ as perfect God and perfect man

Right:
A devil trying to persuade Pilate's wife to stop the crucifixion, and her attempt to induce a busy husband to pay attention to her dream. From the *Hortus Deliciarum* of Herrad of Lansberg, a fourteenth-century text edited by Kellar-Straub at Strasbourg in 1879.
Below:
Fish and loaves as a eucharistic symbol from the crypt of Lucina in the catacombs of St Callistus, Rome.
Below right:
Heracles fighting with the Hydra, as pictured by the Italian Renaissance painter Antonio Pollaiuolo. Heracles, the great hero of classical mythology, successfully accomplished the harrowing of hell.

73

A Russian icon of St Ephrem the Syrian, who
lived in the second half of the fourth century,
with scenes from the life of the saint grouped
around the central figure in what had come to
be the traditional manner. This example would
be difficult to date, but the scenery is Russian,
and no trace of later western influences can yet
be seen. Russian Museum, Leningrad.

is to present him as the one perfectly satisfactory sacrificial
victim. Latin writers also, especially St Augustine, who had
received a good classical education, give the notion of sacrifice
the wide sense of a place of meeting between God and man,
the more perfect as they are more perfectly brought together.
In this context the word propitiatory means no more than
favourable or propitious. It has no necessary connection with
payment to God or Satan. If the sacrifice of Christ covers
some of the same ground in Christ's saving work of rescue as
the harrowing of hell, it is a different story. The stories are not
contradictory, but they ought not to have been confused.

The confusion between them in later Western theology had
nothing to do with St Gregory of Nazianzus, so far as I can
see. It was partly due to a complete loss of contact with pagan
religion, but also due to St Anselm's concern to eliminate the
idea of a price paid to a deceived devil. This notion was all
very well in the market places of the Levant, but repulsive to
the moral sensitivity of an Italian nobleman living in a Norman abbey. Unfortunately in fastening man's redemption
more firmly and exclusively to the sacrifice of Christ on the
cross, he interpreted it in terms of a satisfaction given by way
of ransom to the just judgement of God. This is no longer a
matter of the divine Son's taking a slave's place, but rather of
paying an infinite debt in the infinite suffering of an eternal
person.

St Anselm thought of sacrifice in terms of the sin-offerings
of the Old Testament, where no representation of the god in
the victim is allowed to appear. While he himself insisted that
the sacrifice of Christ is the offering of his perfect humanity
on behalf of sinful man, his treatment of the subject was bound
to suggest to others a clash between the Son's mercy and the
Father's justice, or at any rate between mercy and truth,
righteousness and peace in God himself. This added many
lines of dialogue to mystery plays and to dramatic sermons, but
St Anselm must not be made responsible for them. They arise
from the attempt to incorporate something of his moral insight
into the traditional myth of Christ's combat with the devil,
which he wished to eliminate. Still less should he be made
responsible for the idea that Christ descended into hell to
suffer all the penalties of the damned. This belief, which
became the touchstone of Calvinist orthodoxy in a later age, is
closely connected with developments in the mythology of the
life after death. These will be considered in a later chapter.
The early Christians believed that the general resurrection had
begun, and expected its completion before very long. It is in
this context that we have to see not only the absence of prayers
for the dead in the New Testament and their rare occurrence
in the early Church, but belief in the resurrection of some of
the early saints. To one of these, the mother of Christ and a
mother, no doubt, to some early Christian groups, we must
now turn.

Lives of the Virgin Mary

Little is written in the New Testament about the mother of Jesus, but enough to show that she was a familiar figure in those circles for whom the *Acts of the Apostles* and the Gospels of St Luke and St John were intended. Stories about her fall into two groups: those concerned with her own background and her son's birth, including the accounts of the birth of Jesus in the Gospels of St Matthew and St Luke, and those relating the circumstances of her death and burial, including in some cases her resurrection and assumption into heaven.

Her birth, childhood and dedication

All accounts of the childhood of Mary derive some material, directly or indirectly, from the *Protevangelium* or *Book of James*, so called because the storyteller is supposed to be James, 'the Lord's brother', who appears under that name in the *Acts* and in St Paul's Epistles. Of this book we possess a Greek text assigned by the experts to the third century, but in this very early copy it is already a composite work, with

The meeting of Joachim and Anna after both have heard that Anna is to conceive. Similar pictures are found in illustrations of the *Books of Kings* to represent the conception of a prince. This painting by Giotto is at Padua.
Right:
The Virgin's suitors with their staffs at Odda stave-church, Hardanger, Norway.
Below right:
The annunciation to the Virgin of the birth of Christ, detail from St Bernward's bronze door at Hildesheim.

additions out of tune with the main theme. These multiply in translations into many languages. Many of these additions come from that penumbra between pagan and Christian religion of which something has already been said. The richest and the most varied, but also the wildest, crop of Marian legends springs from Ethiopia, where the penumbra persists. But some additions in the Syriac version look like corrections in the interests of probability, and possibly in the light of information available in Palestine.

The plot of the *Protevangelium* is based on the story of Samuel, who was born to a barren woman in answer to her entreaties. He was presented to the Lord as soon as he was weaned to serve in the sanctuary at Shiloh, where he grew up in a priestly atmosphere until he was called to denounce the sins of the clergy. The name of Anna, Mary's mother, is very close to Samuel's mother, Hannah, and as we shall see Joseph is given a little boy called Samuel. The underlying theme is dedication to virginity from the womb, as seen most probably in a Christian community of widows and virgins, with that tender interest in small babies that is often found in such places. The background is not Jewish, for on points of observance the details are out of focus.

An interesting instance which may throw light on the provenance of the story is the emphasis given to the *petalon*, a plate or flower of gold-leaf on the mitre or turban of the High-priest. This glitters when the sacrifice of Joachim, Mary's father is duly accepted, but reference to the *Talmud* will show that while there is much in Rabbinic lore about this *petalon* or *ziz*, described in *Exodus* 28. 36-38, the point of this is that its propitiatory virtue cannot fail. But Polycrates, Bishop of Ephesus towards the end of the second century, defending Asiatic traditions, recalled in passing that the beloved disciple, to whom Jesus entrusted his mother, had worn a priestly *petalon*. No doubt this shone out over his smiling face to the delight of small children. Polycrates, or more likely his mother, may have been one of them, and another the authoress (or author) of the *Protevangelium*.

The book begins with a very human story of a barren wife preparing for 'the great day of the Lord', and urged by her maid to put off mourning garments and put on a headband which 'the mistress of the work' had given to the maid, who insists: 'It is not fitting for me to wear it, because I am a slave and it bears a royal mark.' Anna was sensitive to the reproach that: 'The Lord God has shut up your womb, to give you no fruit in Israel.' She knew that her husband was charged with neglecting his duty. He could be expected to take a more fruitful second wife, or even to put her away. Nevertheless she consented to wash her hair and to put on festival garments. She went out into the garden in the afternoon and broke out into poetical lamentation beside a laurel bush containing a nest of sparrows. The poetry is not distinguished, but such as might reasonably be attributed to an Ephesian widow or virgin. Birds, animals, waters, earth all bring forth fruit to the glory of God. Anna could not, but her prayer was heard and an angel appeared to tell her that she

would conceive a child who would be spoken of everywhere in the world. Anna in reply offered her baby, whether it were a boy or a girl, to the Lord to serve him always. In the Greek text as it stands this whole scene is preceded by an account of the troubles of Joachim on 'the great day of the Lord', but this is probably an addition. In any case he too had been told by an angel what was to happen, and was preparing a whole set of sacrifices for the coming feast when Anna came out of the house and hung on his neck with her good news. On the next day he offered his gifts, saying to himself: 'If the Lord God is gracious to me, the *petalon* of the priest will declare it to me.' This he observed 'when he went up to the altar of the Lord: and he saw no sin in himself'. (In the Syriac version he saw an encouraging message for him.) This incident could reflect the experience of a Christian taking his communion from someone wearing a *petalon*.

In due course the baby was born and her mother was ritually purified. She nursed her child and called her Mary. The next part of the story is an idyll of maternity, elaborated in some of the versions with poetry. In a Coptic fragment

Left:
Details from Maximian's throne. Above: Mary is made to drink the bitter water, while Joseph, holding his staff, expects the same test, below on the right. Below: an angel tells Joseph not to fear. The same or another angel, also holding a staff, hold the ass still while Joseph helps the Virgin to descend, for her time is at hand.
Right:
The Magi, presented as three kings, visit the infant Jesus and offer the three gifts of gold, frankincense and myrrh. A detail from Pisano's pulpit in the Baptistery of Pisa.
Overleaf:
Further details from St Bernward's door at Hildesheim. The birth of Christ, top, is a very human scene, in which the animals appear in deference to tradition, but Joseph and the midwife are more important. Both mother and child hold out their arms for each other. The three kings (originally the Magi) are seen in the centre picture. The presentation of Christ in the Temple is seen in the bottom picture. The old priest Simeon takes him tenderly from his mother, while Joseph stands in the background with the doves.

'Anna took the baby into her arms to wash her; and she looked down in her face and saw it full of God's grace. She sang this song to the Lord, and David the holy singer replied to her: "The Lord has looked down from heaven on the houses of the poor. He has made them rich. Amen . . . Cherubim of the Father with six wings and four faces, with a thousand eyes full of light, rejoice with me, for I have learnt to make melody for my wise child. Amen. You . . . without bodies, rejoice with me, for a forsaken womb has received a seed." '

Anna is here presented as the proud mother of a precocious but entirely human child. 'Her mother stood her on the ground to see if she could stand, and she walked seven steps and came back to her bosom' (in another version her apron). This is at the age of six months in the Greek. The Syriac version connects the incident with her first birthday. In the Greek there is a birthday party, with priestly guests and blessings. In this version also Mary was taken to the Temple like Samuel at the age of three. She danced for pleasure on the third step of the altar and 'the whole house of Israel loved her'. She remained there with the Temple doves 'fed from the hand of an angel', until she was twelve and her future became a problem for the priests.

Here the Syriac is a good deal more realistic, and may depend on a source with access to some genuine historical information. In this version Mary's mother is sometimes called Dina and sometimes Hanna, and her father Zadok Yonakhir. Mary is indeed a child of promise, promised to God, but she is still living at home at the age of ten. Dina says 'Let us wait until she knows herself, before we take her up.' At about this time another baby, a sister for Mary, is born to the aging pair, and called Paroghitha. At twelve years old Mary is taken to the Temple with seven other virgins and entrusted to the care of an elderly priest called Zadok and his wife Sham'i. She was called the daughter of Zadok 'according to the law of the Lord, but she was rightly and strictly the daughter of Yonakhir by promise'. This must mean that she was adopted, for we are told that 'when twelve years were ended, Yonakhir and his wife Hanna died'. Mary was no more than fourteen when 'Sham'i the wife of Zadok died also'. This in the Syriac version precipitates the crisis that arises in the Greek simply through Mary's adolescence.

The marriage of the Virgin

By this time, in most of the later stories, Mary was living a life of ideal asceticism, fed by angels from the fruits of the tree of life, clad in garments that miraculously grew with her. She always remained neat and tidy although she never put on unguents or had a bath. She was, inevitably, averse to marriage with anyone. But there is nothing of this in the *Protevangelium* except the food from the hand of an angel. The High priest, who is Zacharias, the father of John the Baptist, is advised to enquire of the Lord about her, and is told by an angel in the Holy of Holies that if he would assemble 'the widowers of the people' the Lord would give a sign to the man who should marry her. This is a dove that comes out of Joseph's rod and settles on his head. In the Syriac the miraculous element is greatly reduced. The meeting is indeed held by an angel's order, but it is of men belonging to the royal house of David. The dove is a Temple dove, who perches on Joseph's staff and then on his head. Mary has not been living in the Temple, but with Zadok and Sham'i. She has heard the sound of the angels' praises three times, but nothing is said about angels giving her food. The sense of the meeting is that Joseph is in any case the right person to take charge of her, since he and she 'were each the child of the other's uncle'. He objected that he was elderly, and that 'my wife is the mother of sons and daughters'. We are told that this wife was herself called Mary, and that her sons were Jacob and Jose. In the Syriac she seems to be alive, but in the Greek Joseph is unambiguously a widower. His second son's name is Samuel, sometimes corrected to Joses or to Simon. Nothing is said in either

version of other sons who appear in St Mark's Gospel (6.3) where the brothers of Jesus are James (Jacob), Joses, Judas and Simon.

In both versions Joseph's objections are overcome. He accepted the charge of his little cousin, and took her to his home, either in Jerusalem or in Bethlehem, while he went away on a building job which must have lasted for some time. In the Syriac he was building a house in Bethlehem. Mary was left in Jerusalem, perhaps (although this is not stated) in the charge of the older Mary. If so she was their ward, who was given the status of a wife to protect her name when she conceived a child. This is historically possible, but not mythologically plausible. So Joseph's other wife, if she ever existed, had to be dead. In the Latin infancy gospels she and all Joseph's children are eliminated, and 'the Lord's brethren' turned into cousins, for in the eyes of St Jerome the perpetual virginity of Mary could be maintained only by making Joseph too a dedicated celibate.

By modern scholars Joseph's other wife has been eliminated on other grounds, as an invention to explain Joseph's children without allowing any of them to be Mary's, but some of the evidence does suggest that Jacob or James was an older man than Jesus and his apostles. He took the lead in the church of Jerusalem, where his conservative interpretation of the Christian message made difficulties for St Paul, but for a time won toleration for Jewish Christians from other Jews. Perhaps his mother was Mary, the mother of James and Joses, who watched the passion from a distance in St Matthew's Gospel, was present at the burial of Jesus in St Mark, and appears among the witnesses to the resurrection in St Mark and St Luke. In the Syriac life of the Virgin she is called Mary the wife of Joseph, who in this context is probably Joseph of Arimathea. But a reference to Paroghitha, the sister of Mary, who is identified with the mother of the sons of Zebedee, suggests that the same source is being used as had been followed in the account of Mary's childhood, where Joseph's first wife is also called Mary. It is possible to believe that the mother of James and Joses was Joseph's other wife without taking sides for or against the perpetual virginity of Mary the mother of Jesus, who could have been the mother of some of Joseph's other children. What seems most unlikely is that this appearance of polygamy should be the invention of a Christian Syrian. It could have been taken from a Jewish Christian gospel with information from the families of Judas and Simon.

In the *Protevangelium* Mary and other virgins are given the task of weaving a veil for the Temple. The purple and scarlet fell to her share. She heard a voice at the well calling her highly-favoured, and blessed among women. She looked to the left and right, and saw no one. Trembling, she returned home and put down her pitcher. She took up the purple thread to go on with the job, and suddenly saw the angel by her. She heard him say: 'Don't be afraid, for you have found favour with the Lord of all things, and you will conceive his word'. Her doubts and fears, immediately expressed, were as immediately answered: 'A power of the Lord will come over you. Therefore

what will be born of you will be called holy, the Son of the
Most High.' Mary's reply is given in the words of the Gospel
of St Luke: 'I am the Lord's handmaid. According to your
words so let it be.' She completed her task, received a blessing
from the priest who took it from her, and knocked at the door
of the High priest's wife, her cousin Elizabeth, who was then
expecting a baby, St John the Baptist. Again she received a
warm welcome and a fervent blessing, more than she expected,
for the words of the angel were fading from her memory.

Someone has here inserted 'she remained three months
with Elizabeth' in order to square the story with that in St
Luke, but the original almost certainly continued: 'Day by
day her womb grew and Mary was afraid, and went into her
house and hid herself . . . She was sixteen when these strange
things happened'. The indignation of Joseph, when her plight
was discovered, is expressed in terms of shame that he had left
her not properly protected in his own home. He thought of her
as the little girl who was intimate with the angels, and as she
wept but had no explanation of her condition, he himself
wondered whether they had something to do with it: 'I fear
lest what is in her may have sprung from the angels.' He did
not dare deliver her innocence to the consequences that might
follow a charge of fornication. A dream relieved his immediate
anxieties, for an angel told him that the child was of the Holy
Spirit, but Mary's condition could not be concealed from the
circle of the High priest, to which Joseph as well as Mary is
here represented as belonging. They jumped to the conclusion
that he had consummated his second marriage without the
proper formalities. As he and she both denied this they were
made to drink the bitter water prescribed for a suspected
adulteress in the *Book of Numbers* (5.26). Both went for a
long walk in the country and returned without feeling upset,
which was *prima facie* evidence of their innocence. But this
must be taken as meaning that their marriage, though clandes-
tine, was not condemned by the High priest and his friends.

The birth and infancy of Jesus

The Gospels of St Matthew and St Luke give different
accounts of Jesus' birth, though they agree in the virgin birth
at Bethlehem. The original author of the *Protevangelium* had
evidently read both of them, but felt no obligation to follow
either in detail. The account in St Luke's Gospel was intended
to conflate and harmonise stories about Jesus and St John the
Baptist. Mary is there represented as living in Nazareth,
coming to Emmaus, near Jerusalem, to visit Elizabeth, and to
Bethlehem with Joseph for the census, that their names might
be recorded in the city of David as members of his royal
family. In the *Protevangelium*, as in St Matthew's Gospel,
they belong to Bethlehem. They went for a walk in the country
with Joseph's two boys, Jacob (James) and Samuel, Mary
riding an ass and seeming alternately gay and sad at the
prospect in front of her. They were close to the third mile-
stone when she asked to be taken down, 'for the child within
me presses to come forth'. A cave was found where Mary was
left in the care of the two boys; Joseph went for a midwife.

Since the *Protevangelium* is the *Book of James* we may fairly

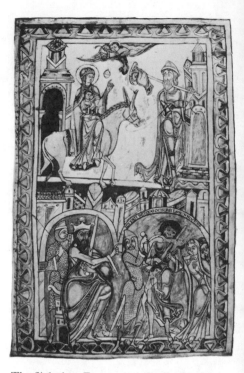

The flight into Egypt, symbolically short and
successful, despite the anxiety of Joseph.
The angel swinging a censer over the Virgin
and her child has his face turned towards them
and his censer receives a blessing from both.
Below, King Herod orders and his soldiers
sadistically execute the massacre of the innocents. Cotton MS Nero c. iv, f. 14 of the
twelfth century. British Museum.
Right:
Christ receives his mother's soul. The South
portal of Strasbourg cathedral, 1250–1260.
Below:
The Death of the Virgin with her coronation
represented over it, on the great portal of the
Virgin at Notre Dame, Paris, 1200–1220.

suppose that in the original text James was there at the climax, doing his best for Mary and the baby, while Samuel stood at the entrance, watching for his father, or went in search of other aid. But in the Greek as we have it, and in all the versions so far as I can discover, the boys have vanished. Perhaps their part was thought improper or indelicate. In the Syriac Joseph returns with an old Hebrew woman coming from Jerusalem. By that time it was dark, but they found the cave full of light and the child, already swaddled, at Mary's breast. 'And while they were wondering at the light some shepherds came and made a great fire, and the heavenly hosts appeared, singing hymns and praising God.' Perhaps in the original Samuel fetched the shepherds, and the child was washed and swaddled in the light of the fire, with the angels there to give the kind of assistance that is often ascribed to them in moments of crisis. But in the Greek as we have it Joseph walks on in a haze. All nature stops and all human actions are arrested for a moment 'and then all at once everything went on its way again'. He met a midwife and explained the situation in what seems unnecessary detail. This could be original, but what follows when they return to the cave comes from another source.

The passage has already been cited in the last chapter to illustrate the idea that Jesus was and is a simply supernatural being. The same idea is found in the *Ascension of Isaiah*, a composite work containing Jewish and Christian materials, whose Christian parts may be older than the *Protevangelium*, since some have found a reference to them in a letter of St Ignatius, written before 110. Here the baby simply materialises while Mary is sitting at home with Joseph, 'and her womb was found as it was before she conceived'. We are left with a strong impression that her pregnancy, which has lasted for two months, is simply a sign to her. That an idea of this kind should be successfully intruded into the *Protevangelium* at the climax – 'that light withdrew until the child appeared, and went and took his mother's breast' – is a forecast of the future of this kind of literature. It is no accident that almost immediately afterwards Salome, who seeks to test the virginity of Mary, has a finger burnt off in the fire. A mountain opens to receive Elizabeth and her son John, so that Herod's soldiers cannot find them, and in the relatively sober Syriac life of Mary the holy family are transported to Egypt in the twinkling of an eye, possibly because the compiler could not imagine any other way of getting there with a newborn baby.

It seems most likely that the original *Protevangelium*, being the *Book of James*, ended with the birth of Jesus; James and Samuel worshipping him by the shepherd's fire, and angels singing behind them. The last chapters of the Greek as they now stand are a clumsy effort to reconcile *St Matthew* with *St Luke* by bringing Elizabeth, Zacharias and St John the Baptist into the story of Herod's massacre of the innocents. This could indeed be founded on some attempt of Herod's to extirpate the remnants of the House of David, but St Matthew did not intend to place it directly after the birth, but at some indefinite date within the first two years. In his presentation of the story the flight into Egypt is a way of explaining the move from Bethlehem to Nazareth. It is also symbolically important, like the visit of the wise men, as a prophetic sign of Christ's future mission to be 'a light for revelation to the Gentiles', as St Luke has it in the song of Simeon at Mary's purification, the corresponding episode in his version of the story.

Several stories of the flight into Egypt make better sense if we suppose the child to be of an age to get down from his mother's lap and order a dragon about. On another occasion sitting on her knee he told a palm tree to bend down and provide fruit for the party. As a reward for obedience a branch from the palm was plucked by an angel and planted in heaven. This fancy is more pleasing than miracles wrought by swaddling bands laid out to dry, but there is a good story of Mary throwing one over a poor demented woman who was about to throw a stone at her. The devil promptly went out of her as she bound the swaddling band round her naked waist and went to make her peace with her family, who received the holy family with honour and gratitude. There are other stories of dumb and deranged women who were healed by embracing, or carrying Jesus, and one of a robber who kidnapped him but brought him back safely. The offensive element lies partly in the magical power ascribed to swaddling bands and bathwater, and partly in the theme of infant omnipotence that runs through so many stories of the boyhood of Christ, in which he

Caravaggio's version of a favourite theme in Christian art. *The Death of the Virgin*, now in the Louvre, was painted in 1606.
Above right:
The Assumption, depicted by Rubens. His angels are very like human children. They may indeed be conceived as baptised innocents, but the spectators are not obviously apostles. They could be any group of bereaved Christians, first confounded by an empty tomb, and then assured of the resurrection. Antwerp Cathedral.

appears as the fulfilment of a small boy's dream of absolute power, lingering on in a mind that has never grown up, a kind of white imp or divine poltergeist.

The death of Mary

This is myth, but of another sort and of a different date, with poetry in it. It revolves round the house church on Mount Sion, in the higher part of Jerusalem, where the upper room of the Last Supper was shown, and downstairs another place where the Holy Spirit came down upon the disciples. This building was enlarged in the middle of the fourth century into a great church containing the place where Christ was said to have received his mother's soul in death. Another focus is a tomb in the valley of the Kedron, close to Gethsemane, where many members of the church of Jerusalem were probably buried. There in the middle of the fifth century a church was built over the empty grave of Mary. The church on Sion and the garden of Gethsemane had been signs and symbols of the early days, not only to the church of Jerusalem, but to others who came to see the scenes of the New Testament long before the opening up of the other holy places.

In the story of her death Mary is the *orante*, the praying Church. Christ came to her in prayer and told her that in three days he would take her away to his heavenly city. She called to her what apostles were available, and then the virgins of the church of Jerusalem, ordered her own grave-clothes, with spices and perfumes, told the virgins to light the lamps as the evening came, then prayed at some length and lay down to die. Christ came for her straightaway, riding in the chariot of the Cherubim, and her soul leapt into his arms.

In some of the later versions all the apostles are gathered from their fields of mission, St John from Ephesus, St Peter from Rome, St Matthew from on board ship somewhere in the Mediterranean, St Andrew, St Mark and St Luke from their graves. All fly through the air in a chariot of light to this general meeting in the upper room on Mount Sion. In all the versions the apostles, or some of them, carry the body of Mary to the grave 'in the valley of Jehoshaphat', but a hostile party meet them and try to burn it. Foiled at first, they renew their attack on the grave itself. In what may be the oldest of the Coptic versions Christ has told his mother that her body will be hidden 'until the day of my coming, and I will raise it incorruptible. But a sweet smell shall be given forth round it until the day it shall rise . . . A lordly shrine shall be built . . . better than the palaces of kings'. This may be the church in Gethsemane, or it may be the language of metaphor, with the visible Church in mind. There is probably some hidden meaning in the seven months that intervene in other Coptic versions between the funeral and Mary's body being taken to heaven. In one version Christ told her that if she had been translated directly there, like Elijah in his chariot of fire, 'wicked men will think that you are a power from heaven'. In the time that elapsed between her death and resurrection (206 days in this version) we may see an echo of older Egyptian ideas of the time required before a soul is established in another form in the other world.

In the older version already quoted, the idea that 'she was taken up in her body to heaven' is directly condemned, as is also the notion that 'the Virgin was not born as we are'. The idea that she was a heavenly being has left few traces except in Ethiopia, but it is found in two rather different forms in two quotations from *The Gospel of the Hebrews*, a Jewish Christian work that seems to have originated in the early second century, and had some currency in Egypt in the third. In one of the quotations Christ speaks of 'my mother the Holy Spirit taking me up by one of my hairs'. In another Mary is identified with a heavenly power called Michael: 'And the power came into the world and was called Mary, and Christ was in her womb seven months'. The influence of such ideas may be seen in later versions of the story in which the funeral and the assumption come closer together. Sometimes they fuse and give rise to a suspicion that in the fracas on the way to the funeral the body went up in smoke. But I do not believe that myths about

The Jesse Tree, in Cotton MS Nero c. iv, f. 9.
British Museum.
Right:
The coronation of the Virgin by the three persons of the Holy Trinity, a painting by Velasquez at the Prado in Madrid.

the assumption arise from a confused recollection of such an incident. Rather they spring from a conviction that in the blessed Virgin Mary the resurrection is a present reality, that the first fruits of the Church in her are in the heavens.

Those who framed lives of the Virgin clearly believed in her perpetual virginity. It is not so evident that they had any special interest in her conception, but the story of the *petalon* suggests that a sense of innocence was thought appropriate to Mary's parents on this occasion in the second century. Their embrace, where this is figured, follows older models in the biographies of gods and heroes. A sermon of St Gregory Palamas in the fourteenth century explores the idea of a remnant of the elect children of God who can be traced through the Virgin's ancestors from Seth to Enoch and King David. This idea has no particular connection with St Augustine's ideas of original sin, of which this St Gregory probably knew little or nothing. The Virgin of the *Protevangelium* is rather to be conceived as the perfectly innocent child, the little girl who could be terribly afraid, but never sinned.

St Peter in the Baptistery of the Orthodox, built in the fifth century at Ravenna.
Below:
St Peter with a soldier on the sarcophagus of Junius Bassus (A.D. 359). The Vatican, Rome.
Below right:
Two scenes from an ivory casket of the early fifth century. Above: St Peter raises Dorcas from the dead (*Acts* 9. 36–40). Below: Thecla listens to St Paul, who reads from a scroll. On the right St Paul is being stoned, perhaps at Lystra (*Acts* 14. 14–19). British Museum.

Lives of the saints

Apocryphal Acts of the Apostles

The Acts of the Apostles in the New Testament have some of the characteristics of a popular adventure, hairbreadth escapes from prison and death, difficult journeys, visits to places of interest like Athens, Ephesus and Rome, a shipwreck described in considerable detail, but there is no love interest, and the conclusion is an anti-climax: St Paul is left in Rome under house arrest for two years without trial or martyrdom. The *Apocryphal Acts* attempt to remedy these deficiencies. *The Acts of Paul* had certainly been in circulation for some time at the end of the second century, in a form compiled, according to Tertullian, by a presbyter of a church in Asia, who wrote them 'for love of Paul', but was deposed for his pains. They are now believed to depend on an early form of the *Acts of Peter*. Both record the martyrdom of the two apostles in the persecution that followed the great fire in Rome in A.D. 64, not long after the imprisonment of St Paul as recorded in *Acts* 28. Both also assume that St Paul was released in time for a spell of adventure in Spain and elsewhere.

The Acts of Paul and Thecla

In this episode St Paul appears on the scene coming into Iconium from Lystra, 'a short man with a bald head and bandy legs, but strongly built, with a long nose, eyebrows meeting over this, and a striking expression. Sometimes he seemed just a man, but at other times had the face of an angel'. Onesiphorus was looking out for him, having heard of him from Titus, and took him and his companions into his house, where there was much talk 'of self-control and the resurrection'. A young lady called Thecla listened from a window next

door. She was engaged to a young man called Thamyris, but probably reluctant to commit herself to marriage, for she paid special attention to what St Paul had to say about virginity. To her mother's great indignation she went on eavesdropping, and would not turn round even when kissed by her betrothed. Thamyris was hurt, and decided to investigate. He was fortunate enough to find disciples of the saint who had fallen out with him on the subject of the resurrection. On their information he charged him with being a magician who made virgins averse to marriage. His charges were supported by much popular clamour, and St Paul was put into ward until the governor (a proconsul, as in Asia) should have time to consider the case. Thecla, however, by bribing the porter and the jailor, got into the prison, where she sat at his feet and kissed his chains.

At his trial she kept on looking at him. He was simply scourged and expelled from the city, but her own mother demanded that Thecla should be burnt as an example to other deluded girls. The governor consented and her execution was immediately arranged, other young men and women piling up faggots for the fire. She looked around and thought she saw Paul, but what she really saw was the Christ, who went up into heaven before her eyes. She made the sign of the cross as she mounted the pyre, but the fire did not burn, for an earthquake began, a cloudburst followed, the fire was quenched in rain, and Thecla found herself free.

In the original story this may have been the climax. Thecla was to be burnt as a witch, but her martyr's baptism of blood and fire was stopped and then completed by another baptism in rain from heaven. In the text as we have it we are not told what happens next, for the scene shifts to a tomb some way from the town where St Paul had taken refuge with Onesiphorus and his whole family. One of the boys, sent back to buy provisions, met Thecla in the market place at Iconium, apparently shopping (but was she living at home?) and told her that Paul had been praying for her for six days. She came back with him to the tomb, and shared their frugal meal. St Paul was glad of her escape, but did not approve her intention to cut off her hair and follow him, fearing that she might be running into a worse temptation, and fall. She asked for the seal of baptism, but he told her to wait in patience until she should 'receive the water'. This happens in circumstances which have nothing to do with St Paul and may be taken from the acts of another martyr.

Thecla followed him to Antioch in Syria, where he denied any connection with her. She was thrown to the beasts for tearing the cloak and garland of a man of some distinction who tried to make love to her, but the lions and bears either refused to touch her or devoured one another. She baptised herself in a pool full of fighting seals, who were struck by lightning as she plunged in. She was tied to maddened bulls, who broke their cords and rushed in opposite directions. Finally she was released at the instance of a great lady who had already taken an interest in her. My own conjecture is that in the original story this lady received her, perhaps at another

Joachim and Anna with the High Priest, looking at the *petalon* in his mitre. This is a detail from the right-hand lancet of the window at Le Mans Cathedral shown in full on page 25.

The presentation of the Virgin in the Temple. She mounts the steps of the altar, supported by her father, while her mother remains modestly behind. From the right-hand lancet of the window at Le Mans Cathedral shown in full on page 25.

Antioch in Pisidia, after the attempt to burn her at Iconium had failed. After converting her whole household she turned her tunic into a man's cloak and went in search of St Paul. She found him at Myra in Lycia, where he gave her a warmer welcome than he did at the tomb. She told him the story of her baptism (of blood and fire and rain, or with seals in the water?) and announced her intention of going back to Iconium, to which St Paul replied: 'Go, and teach the word of God'. Thamyris was dead, and her mother would not hear her, and so she went to Seleucia where she lived for a number of years, in some versions to the age of seventy-two.

Additions to her story take the form of ascetic achievements, healing miracles and, if I am right about Antioch, escapes from wild beasts. As the Great Church took a firmer line about the limits of the New Testament, much of this apocryphal literature was preserved in sects that had deviated from it in one direction or another. Some of these deviations are associated with the 'Docetic' or 'Gnostic' atmosphere that we have already encountered in *The Ascension of Isaiah* and in some additions to lives of the Virgin. But in the Acts in particular it is difficult to distinguish between sectarian additions, orthodox corrections made when the books were later claimed by the Church for purposes of edification and entertainment, and the original shape of the tale. The emphasis on virginity for instance is often ascribed to doctrinal extravagance, but it may have more to do with the romantic interest. Married Christians who stayed at home were less liable to hairbreadth escapes, nor were they so dramatically torn between the love of Christ and family affections. This especially applies to marriages broken by the conversion of one partner but not the other. These could, but need not, imply a low estimate of married life, which is always difficult to describe favourably in fiction.

St Peter and Simon Magus

In a number of stories one or more of the apostles are brought into conflict with Simon, the Samaritan magician who made a fleeting appearance in *Acts* 8. According to Justin Martyr, who had himself lived in Samaria, he was the founder of the Simonians, a sect still powerful there in the middle of the second century, and he himself had come to Rome in the time of the Emperor Claudius. This was before St Peter or St Paul could have arrived, and Justin says nothing of their conflicts with Simon. But where Simonians and Christians were in controversy it was natural to introduce the idea of a competition in Rome between the two Simons, Peter and the magician ('Magus'). Some of these competitions are fantastic. A dog and a baby act as messengers from St Peter to Simon, the dog barking and the baby crying invectives at him. Simon succeeded in getting a dead boy to raise his head, but St Peter made him get up, put on his clothes, and give an account of his experiences. Hippolytus, at the beginning of the third century, tells a story that Simon was buried alive at his own request, but failed to rise. In the *Acts of Peter* he took off from a tower and flew over the forum in the city of Rome, but fell suddenly and broke his bones as his diabolical machinery failed him, and he died soon afterwards.

St Paul in the church of St Vitale, built in the middle of the sixth century at Ravenna.
Right:
St Paul in the Archiepiscopal oratory of St Andrew at Ravenna, where the mosaics date from about 500.
Far right:
St Paul in the Arian baptistery of the sixth century at Ravenna.

Because some of these stories reflect the views of Jewish Christians hostile to St Paul, it has been held that the whole idea of a competition for power between St Peter and Simon is really a reflection of struggles between these Jewish Christians and St Paul's disciples, and indeed that Simon is really St Paul in disguise. These stories are set in the narrative framework of the troubles of Clement, a Roman convert from a distinguished family, who has lost touch with his mother and twin brothers, and then with his father's search for his mother. The situation was in the common stock of popular literature in a world where slavery broke up families, and babies were frequently exposed, but occasionally fostered, and might be recovered by 'tokens of recognition'.

In the Greek version called *The Clementine Recognitions*, enlarged and developed in some editions into what is called *The Clementine Homilies*, the battle between Simon and St Peter is fought in the haunts of Jewish Christians, at Caesarea, Tripoli and Antioch. In the course of these controversial developments Clement found his lost relations. An Arabic version, less burdened with disputations, brings him back with St Peter to Rome. In all the stories he is identified with a Clement who owed his historical reputation to his leadership in the Roman church at the end of the first century and the beginning of the second. Whatever his precise relationship to the family of Flavius Clemens, a disgraced aristocrat suspected of Jewish superstition, in whose household he may have been a slave and then a freedman, the historical Clement played an important role in a predominantly Gentile church. He could well have been the narrator in an early Roman version of the *Acts of Peter*, but it is difficult to see why Jewish Christians hostile to St Paul should make up a story about him. They probably inserted their own homiletic materials into an older 'adventures of St Peter and Clement with Simon Magus'. I do not believe that all the other stories about the missions of the apostles were invented to put St Paul into the shade.

Foundation stories

Other apocryphal acts circulated chiefly in the east. Some of them, like the *Acts of Andrew and Matthias in the city of the cannibals*, and the *Acts of Peter and Andrew*, where St Peter puts a camel through a needle's eye, were probably preserved primarily to vindicate the claims of particular churches to apostolic foundation. Some of these churches were outside the civilised world of the Roman empire, and in their isolation had developed more or less important deviations in doctrine and practice from what was normal there. The church of Edessa in Persian Mesopotamia treasured not only the *Acts of Thaddaeus*, but a letter written by Prince Abgar, the ancestor of the Christian dynasty of Osrhoene, to Christ himself. The *Acts of Bartholomew* had a like value to the national church of Armenia. The *Acts of Thomas*, composed at Edessa, came to be treasured by the Syrian Christians of Malabar as their authority for the story that the Apostle St Thomas had been in India, although the India of this legend, telling of a carpenter engaged to build a king's palace, who built a palace in heaven for the king by his charities, is certainly not Malabar, and may not be in the Indian peninsula. Curiously enough, however, some of the materials read as if they may have been borrowed from Buddhists, and in a *Gospel of Thomas*, belonging to the same collection, traces of Buddhist sources have been found.

On the other hand the moving accounts of the martyrdom in Rome of St Peter and St Paul, including St Peter's meeting with Christ, his question: 'Where are you going?', the answer: 'I go to Rome to be crucified again', and the outcome in the crucifixion of the prince of the apostles upside down, became more and more important to the Roman church as the city ceased to be the effective capital of the empire, and therefore the only conceivable centre from which any society operating everywhere in the civilised world could be organised. It was then that Rome, the old capital of the empire, came to be first and foremost the apostolic see, founded by St Peter and St Paul, and treasuring their trophies and remains. Some of the prestige of the *Clementine Recognitions* and of some other apocryphal acts with St Peter involved in them, among some Protestant historians, is almost certainly due to the desire to

St Francis renouncing his inheritance from his father before the Bishop of Assisi. One of a sequence of frescoes made by Giotto to illustrate the life of St Francis in the church built to commemorate him at Assisi soon after his death in 1226.

keep St Peter out of Rome. On the other hand Roman Catholic authorities have shown a like concern to turn trophies into tombs. The places where the martyrs died were centres of a cult some time before an interest in their bones very naturally developed.

The passions of martyrs and others

A few accounts of early Christian martyrs depend in part on official reports of their interrogation before the magistrates or on the direct testimony of eyewitnesses. A good many more may have been composed with the help of earlier accounts of this kind, but transformed by the exercise of the devout imagination into historical novelettes. A quite considerable class of acts and passions of the martyrs are in effect creations of the hagiographer's art, working on at most a name, a tomb, and a day of commemoration, and often on a tomb without a name, or a local feast that must be transferred from a god or nymph to a saint or saints.

In such accounts the magistrates, who in authentic records are above all anxious to secure recantations from deluded innocents, are transformed into monsters thirsting for blood. The accusers are an infuriated mob. The martyr generally makes a magnificent speech, adorned with as many rhetorical figures and philosophical tags as are available to the hagiographer. The first attempts to kill him or her nearly always fail. They are generally followed by refined tortures, but the martyr remains capable of reproaching his captors and inspiring his friends with eloquent prayers.

After the martyrs the holy virgins, the hermits and monks of the desert, and the good abbot acquired their characteristic legends. No doubt in many cases some material was available to their hagiographers, perhaps enough to make a sufficiently interesting story, but gaps required to be filled. A number of saints were the subject of dreams while they were still in the womb or before they were conceived. Many gave presages of their fame as small children, by lamenting in Lent or refusing food on fastdays. The ladies introduced into their rooms to try their chastity may prove to have been borrowed from another saint's biography. Even where the substance of a saint's life is clearly his own reminiscences, as in the very interesting life of St Cyril the Phileote—who had been a peasant farmer, a sailor and a maker of ropes, and a married man with at least two children, before he lost his beloved wife in an invasion and became a monk in about 1050—the conversations contain much that is lifted, with and without acknowledgment, from philosophers and Christian Fathers who could express themselves in better Greek. Among the sources cited by name are Aristotle, Plato, Antisthenes and Diogenes, but much more has come from Epictetus, a Stoic of the second century, by way of a standard monastic manual composed in the fifth or sixth century.

It must be remembered that in the medieval as in the ancient world biography was a branch of rhetoric. Lives of the saints were meant to be read aloud for purposes of edification. They had to read well. In the *Acts of Peter with Simon* the dog's invective could be rendered like barking and the baby's

In this picture of a debate between the Apostles and Simon Magus the Emperor Nero is conceived in terms of a medieval king with ecclesiastical patronage. Simon represents the sin of 'simony'. In his left hand is a bag of money with which, or with services rendered, he is prepared to assist King Nero. St Peter represents ecclesiastical authority, in need at this point of theological assistance from St Paul. A mosaic in the Palatine chapel at Palermo, one of those added by the Aragonese kings of Sicily in the fourteenth century.
Right:
The young Nero. The first active persecution of the Christians took place during the reign of this emperor.
Far right:
The church of San Paolo fuori le mura (St Paul outside the walls) in Rome, built near the spot where St Paul was believed to have suffered martyrdom.

like crying. That does not mean that such works are historically valueless, but their value often lies in the light they throw on aspects of social history. In the *Pratum Spirituale* of John Moschus, who lived in Palestine in the early seventh century, we read of a holy man who got up at night to plough a poor neighbour's field and sow it with his own seedcorn, who carried weary children up the steep road from Jericho to Jerusalem, and always had in his pockets the tools he needed to mend other people's shoes. We also hear of a monk who fed birds with biscuits and gave flour to the small ants and grain to the big ones. Not all the stories are so edifying: some in the same book are very odd, like one about a ship that would not move until a mother who owned to having murdered two of her children was safely drowned; but all throw some light on actual beliefs and standards of morality. These lives have often been used effectively by unbelieving historians like the late Professor J. B. Bury, who wrote an excellent book on *The Life of St Patrick*. It is interesting to observe that those who do not believe in miracles may often judge their authorities by their responsibility and restraint in recording the miraculous.

Chivalry and the Holy Grail

Perhaps the most interesting saints from the point of view of mythology are those who have inherited characteristics from pagan gods and heroes. It is most likely that St George was a Christian soldier, who tore down a placard in Nicomedia at the beginning of the persecution of Diocletian. Mounted on

horseback as the patron saint of army officers, he acquired possession of a number of symbolic scenes, many of them no doubt of pagan origin, but some of them certainly made by Christians who preferred symbolic to representational art. The mounted Christ or the mounted saint in combat with a dragon was originally conceived as a representation of the battle with sin and the discomfiture of the devil, modelled no doubt in many cases on older representations of the creator and preserver of the world in combat with chaos. In course of time St George became the typical champion of distressed maidens in trouble with dragons, like Perseus who rescued Andromeda, sacrificed by her father to a devouring monster of the deep.

The myth of St George encouraged the chivalrous knight to believe that he could become a saint without becoming a monk or a hermit, if he could only find a damsel in real distress and rescue her from the tyrannical freebooter who might even have succeeded in forcing her into marriage. Differences of opinion as to the validity of the marriage bond in such cases brought many chivalrous knights into conflict with the Church, especially in the south of France, where the cult of chivalry and love developed into sophisticated literary forms in the twelfth and thirteenth centuries.

Here it is necessary to distinguish between the literary use of mythical themes, the probable background of symbols used in these themes in pagan religions of fertility, and their use in Christian mythology. That some symbolism with sexual

associations should appear in pagan and again in Christian
religion is not in the least surprising. We must remember however that the authors of romantic lays had nothing like our
knowledge of the history of Celtic or Greek mythology. They
took their symbols from a store of folktales developed under
Christian influences by peoples whose imagination was still
subconsciously pagan.

A good example of Christian mythology which lies outside
the cycles of romance may be found in the peregrinations of St
Cuthbert's bones from place to a place in the north of England
after the burning of Lindisfarne by the Northmen until
their final establishment at Durham. The bearers of the bones
are always monks, but they are identified by their names and
by some of their characteristics as ancestors of northern
families who in that perilous time had taken church property
under their care at Hexham and elsewhere. The 'foxy' characteristics of the particular family who held firmly to Hexham
until the twelfth century are satirised by the transformation of
their progenitor Eilaff into a fox, for stealing an excellent
cheese from the rest of the **brethren.**

The story of the Holy Grail must have grown in a like time
of devastation. Priests who could sing mass were very rare in
the ninth and tenth centuries in many parts of Western Europe.

Christ bringing up Adam and Eve from the grave to join the saints, who are here represented in full force. Below the gates of hell are flung apart and all instruments of torture are broken. Christ's hands and feet bear no visible wounds. Painted on plaster about 1305 at Kahrie Cami (the Church of St Mary in Chora), Istanbul.
Right:
The martyrdom of St Sebastian, painted in 1475 by Antonio Pollaiuolo, a Florentine (1429–98), with the assistance of his brother Piero. National Gallery, London.

Shrines and churches were preserved and controlled by landed families whose womenfolk were no doubt especially concerned for the holiness of times and places. I would suggest that somewhere, perhaps in several places in the British isles or in the west of France, the custom of keeping the reserved eucharist at home in a holy cup was retained or revived.

Of this mysterious cup, tended by a maiden, all stood in awe but few could understand its use or meaning. It had been for communion and something might still be there of the Body and Blood of Christ, but in the absence of a priest no one knew for certain what should be done with it.

Here we have the potentiality of a very powerful symbol. If the use of the chalice could be rediscovered and the supply of the blessed sacrament replenished, the lost contact with the sacramental life on the mystical Body of Christ would be

98

restored, and the hope of order and healing might return to the kingdom, represented in all versions of the story by a wounded king, sometimes with an aged father. The wound could be healed and the king's health and youth restored, if the knight who came on the quest of the Holy Grail would ask the right questions about its meaning and use. That the dilemma should be expressed in terms of a wound in the king's thighs, and of a wasted land where no crops could grow, the solution in terms of a meeting between male and female symbols, of the Grail in the hands of a maid or maidens, itself containing a lance that drips with blood, and awaiting the lance of the knight, is just what we should expect from our present understanding of the role of sexual symbolism in religion.

But the Grail is a Christian and a eucharistic symbol. It may have affinities with the cauldron of plenty in Celtic mythology, but there is no reason to look for its immediate antecedents in a witch's brew.

Miss Jessie Weston in her various works, *The Legend of Sir Perceval*, *The Quest of the Holy Grail*, and *From Ritual to Romance*, maintained that somewhere in western Europe, probably in Wales, fertility rites were performed on which the prosperity of the land was held to depend – until the priestesses of the cult were insulted by some rough chieftain and his men. After this the rites continued in secret strongholds, where traditions lingered derived from the worship of Isis, from Mithraism, or from some form of Christian Gnosticism. Tales based on these rites were told by the Welsh poet Bleheris to his friends and allies after the Norman conquest in a form that spread like wildfire through western Europe after 1100. The Christian associations of the legend were due to a group of minstrels connected with the Norman abbey of Fécamp, where there was a relic of the blood of Christ.

The cult connected with this relic, which seems to have begun in the first half of the eleventh century, was of a kind that might have arisen from reverence for the reserved eucharist in a place where priests were lacking, and I should be inclined to give the same explanation to the legend of two cruets of Christ's blood and sweat, buried at Glastonbury. The links observed by Miss Weston and others between the quest for the Grail and rituals of initiation into pagan mysteries may be explained by survivals from tribal initiations in Wales and Ireland, or by the influence of the Albigensians on the poetry of Provence.

Provençal influence on the story of the Grail is probable in any case. Wolfram von Eschenbach, whose *Parzival* is the second oldest version of the tale, said that he found it in a poem by Kiot of Provence, which Chrétien de Troyes, the author of the oldest known *Conte du Graal*, had mishandled. In Wolfram's poem the Grail is a stone, guarded by celibate initiates. The Albigensians or Cathars had such an inner circle, the only fully initiated members of their religion, to guard traditions brought to them by refugees from Bulgaria and Byzantium. These had inherited mysteries from other refugees, coming into the Byzantine empire from the Moslem

Above
The vision of the crucified St Peter appearing to Peter Nolasco, the saint who devoted his life to the rescue of Christian captives from the Moors and founded the Order of Our Lady of Ransom. From the painting by Francisco de Zurbarán.
Below:
St Louis of France as depicted in stained glass in terms probably intended to commemorate the passion of King Louis XVI, in the French Revolution. Nineteenth century, Bourges Cathedral.

and Persian east, who in the seventh century started the Paulician movement, deeply coloured by the Gnostic penumbra between Christianity and paganism that we have encountered earlier.

Albigensians certainly contributed something to the legends that locate the graves of Lazarus, whom Christ brought back from the dead, and of his sisters Martha and Mary in the south of France from the thirteenth century, but not before. The story of Joseph of Arimathea, who came with them from Palestine some thirty years after the crucifixion, bringing the Holy Grail used at the Last Supper could come from a similar source. But it seems to be older and its local connections are with Brittany and Cornwall, not with Provence and Languedoc. In the middle of the thirteenth century it was taken up at the Abbey of Glastonbury, which already prided itself on being a centre and shrine of British Christianity before the English arrived. It may be that the story of Joseph of Arimathea and his son Joseph was originally invented in the interests of the Welsh and the Cornish, who wished to claim that their Christianity came directly from Palestine, not from Rome.

It is important that in all these stories the meaning of the Grail is mysterious. It can be recovered only by a knight qualified to ask the right questions about it. I do not think that this symbolises a lost fertility rite. The Christian mystery itself is in question, the chalice as seen through a screen by minstrels who attended mass, but rarely made their confession and communion, and only communicated in the single element of bread.

St Francis and Dante

That the mythological imagination was still very much alive in the thirteenth century is clear from the involved stories of the life of St Francis. The idea that the life of a saint should be modelled on the life of Christ was not a new one. The passions of martyrs were always conceived as conforming to Christ's passion, and often the way that led to them was marked by trials and temptations comparable with his. But in the case of St Francis his call to the apostolic life came to him in the words of the gospel at mass: 'As you go, preaching, saying, the kingdom of heaven is at hand. Heal the sick, cleanse the lepers, raise the dead, cast out devils: freely you have received, freely give . . . ' This commandment led him to go immediately to the lepers and tend their sores, and inevitably compelled him as well as his followers to interpret their imitation of Christ and his apostles in the most direct and literal way, which came to a culmination in his last years when his hands and feet were found to be stamped with Christ's wounds. By that time the movement that he began had grown too large for his limited powers of organisation, and was indeed becoming a religious order of a new kind, such as his older contemporary, St Dominic, had clearly conceived and envisaged. St Francis had seen a vision of the apostolic way of life, but in this there was no place for a new organisation. He was generally, though not invariably, prepared to comply with the requirements of ecclesiastical authority, but he had no notion of making his

little band a part of the Church's machinery of government.

His biographers, however, were concerned either with the foundation of the Franciscan order, or with the contrast between his handful of early disciples and the four orders of friars as they had become by the end of the thirteenth century. The official lives, two by Thomas of Celano, and two, the major and minor, by St Bonaventura, a great scholastic theologian and a greater restorer of peace and harmony within the Franciscan order, were widely circulated as soon as they were written. The longer *Legenda* by St Bonaventura, with an appendix on miracles, was the basis of most of our knowledge about St Francis until the end of the nineteenth century, when more and more material began to be printed in forms that had circulated among the critics of the order's institutional development, who attributed all their favourite stories about the saint to a small group of his immediate disciples.

It is likely enough that some of these stories were found in collections prepared, used and stored at the time when the official lives were written, and some may well have come from Brother Leo, the most literate of the early companions of the saint, but many more reflect much later struggles. They ascribe to St Francis a kind of fundamentalism about the absolute inspiration of the original rule which is not at all in character with the humility of the 'little poor man'. They also reflect controversies that began long after his time. A good example is the story at the beginning of the collection called *The Mirror of Perfection* about the novice who wanted St Francis to approve of his having a psalter. 'And the Blessed Francis said to him: After you have had a psalter, you will be covetous and desire to have a breviary. And when you have a breviary you will sit in a stall like a great prelate and say to your brother "bring me the breviary".' The story goes on to

Some martyrs and confessors represented in the *Hours of Anne de Bretagne*, an illuminated office-book made for Anne of Brittany, the queen successively of Charles VIII and Louis XII of France, by Jean Bourdichon in 1500–1508. MS Latin 9474 in the Bibliothèque Nationale, Paris. Above: The martyrdom of the Theban legion, a lurid tale of the crucifixion of a number of soldiers martyred at Agaunum in the valley of the Rhone, for refusing to take part in a sacrifice for success in the suppression of a revolt of the peasants against heavy taxation and forced labour. They themselves had been raised in Upper Egypt, where there was much discontent of the same sort, and many of the peasants were becoming Christians at the end of the third century. Above centre: St Margaret or Marina of Antioch in Pisidia, with the many-coloured dragon who appeared to her in prison. There may well have been such a person, but her acts are entirely legendary. Left: The conversion of St Hubert, while hunting in the Ardennes on Good Friday, from horse and hound to the ecclesiastical life. The stole offered to him by the angel was one later provided by the Blessed Virgin for his consecration to the see of Tongern, which he himself moved to Liége, where he died in 727. The real turning point in his life was the death of his wife in 685, leaving him with a young son. But he is here apparelled as the patron of huntsmen, in sporting gear of the late fifteenth century.

The mounted Christ conceived in a form
which became the model for later representations of the conflict with evil, carved at Apa
Schenoute, Sohag, in Upper Egypt. Staatliche
Museum, Berlin.

tell how St Francis took ashes from the hearth around which
they were sitting and sprinkled them on his own head 'and
drawing his hand over his head in a circle like one who washes
his head he kept on saying "I a breviary, I a breviary".'

Nothing at first sight could be more characteristic of St
Francis than this story. Nevertheless the Franciscan sisters,
the Poor Clares, in their mother house at Assisi, are in possession of a breviary which according to their tradition had
been used by St Francis and his most intimate companions.
Critical investigation has shown that it must have been made
for a canon or chaplain in some church in or near Rome, but
at some distance from the Lateran, after 1213–16 but before
1222–3. It came into the possession of St Francis and his
companions when it was nearly but not quite new, and it
contains additions in several places in a hand that can be
identified as Brother Leo's. It is certainly one of the oldest, if
not the oldest breviary in existence, in the sense of a book
containing all the materials to be used at the seven canonical
hours of prayer, and it is beyond all question the oldest portable breviary that could be carried away for recitation in
solitude by the wayside.

In the time of St Francis such books were very rare. They
were chiefly found among the clerks of the Roman curia,
whose business kept them continually on the move, and
perhaps here and there in such places as Roman basilicas and
cathedrals in and around Rome. No parish priest had one.
They kept their vigils as well as they could, if devoutly
inclined with a psalter learnt by heart and remembered, and
with some book of lections, Biblical or otherwise. Graduals
and antiphonaries with music for festal and penitential varia-
tions were very rare outside the great churches, cathedrals,
colleges of secular canons, and monasteries, until the friars

arrived with their portable breviaries, suitable for recitation on
the road. Soon parish priests began to want one. Some friars
no doubt did a roaring trade for the order in them. Others
murmured: 'What would St Francis have thought of this?'
No doubt the saint was pleased with anything so convenient
as the breviary given or left to him and his companions by
some clerical friend of theirs. He never imagined that such a
thing would ever be in general circulation. Indeed some early
Franciscan houses moved in the other direction and had their
office books large enough for the whole choir to see and sing
from the same page at the same time, but these could not be
carried on mission.

The circulation of breviaries was one among many signs of
the coming of a literate civilisation. Printing, after this, was
bound to appear, and with it some decline in the reflective
assimilation of what is learnt by heart and pondered. The
mystical interpretation of Scripture was not yet on the way
out, but it was losing its primacy in the Christian life. Dante,
like the Franciscans, stands on the watershed between two
worlds. *The Divine Comedy* contains so much natural scenery
that it can be taken as an essay in terrestrial and celestial
geography. But Dante himself, in his letter to Can Grande,
makes his own intention plain. He is writing mythology in the

The Apostles were a favourite subject of the artists of the Renaissance. On the left is Raphael's *St Paul preaching in Athens*, a cartoon for a later tapestry. On the right is Dürer's *St John and St Peter*. Interestingly, the German artist does not endow his saints with the familiar halo.
Below:
In this icon of St George and the Dragon the child on the crupper is a figure of the Christ whom we see in distressed children. The familiar princess awaits the outcome with complete confidence but her parents are more anxious–though her father proffers a pair of keys as an appropriate reward for his daughter's rescuer. The port of Beirut is on the right. Icon of the second half of the nineteenth century attributed to M.M. al-Qudsi, at Saida in the Lebanon.

same sense as Plato and Virgil, and (in his own view) St Paul. He writes of what he has seen but cannot relate. 'He has not knowledge, because he has forgotten; and he has not power, because if he remembered and retained the matter, nevertheless language fails: for we see many things by the intellect for which there are no vocal signs, of which Plato gives sufficient hint in his books by having recourse to metaphors; for he saw many things by intellectual light which he could not express in direct speech.' He compares this with St Paul's experience told of as 'a man in Christ' in *II Corinthians* 12. 2–3. with the vision of the transfiguration, and with Nebuchadnezzar's dream in the *Book of Daniel*; and for the interpretation of such experiences refers to Richard of St Victor, St Augustine and St Bernard. The explicit reference is to the *Paradise,* but we need not doubt that the poet has the whole of the *Divine Comedy* in mind. He did not claim an inspiration equal to that of the apostles and prophets, but one comparable with theirs, that power of natural prophecy, which in his view, as in that of St Thomas Aquinas, is given to some who are very far from beings saints. The next chapter is about such visions.

104

Below:
The ascension of Antoninus and Faustina,
carried into heaven by a winged genius, while a
personification of Rome makes a gesture of
respect. This illustrates something of the background of ideas of the afterlife in the second
century A.D. It is at the base of the column of
Antoninus Pius in Rome.

Below right:
Illustration from the Beatus Apocalypse,
Spanish of the eleventh century. MS 644, f. 115
v. Pierpont Morgan Library, New York.

Overleaf:
Another illustration of the day of judgement
from an Apocalypse of the thirteenth century.
Trinity College Library, Cambridge.

Visions of the afterlife

Neither Jews nor Greeks had a generally accepted articulated doctrine of life after death. The Jewish Sheol, the land of the dead, was as dim as the Greek Hades, where the shades might be quickened into renewed life by the blood of a sacrifice, but faded again into an undefined host of the dead ancestors. In this they were more like the Babylonians than the Egyptians, but all the peoples of the ancient world, like Africans now, were aware of ancestors, not just as memories but as present powers, who might stand on their feet as a great army. Ideas of individual immortality began to circulate among Jews and Greeks in the sixth and fifth centuries, as the rise of the Persian empire encouraged the diffusion of ideas from Egypt, and perhaps from India. The idea that the soul is immortal by nature logically involves pre-existence as well as persistence

after death, and in this form was advanced by Pythagoras and Plato, as well as by later Platonists, some of whom were almost certainly open to Indian influences.

Some other Greeks, like the Orphics, and probably other adherents of mystery religions, held that immortality is a gift to initiates. The Christians were like them in that they began from the resurrection as a gift given by Christ of new life in him and in the fellowship of the Holy Spirit, to those who were prepared to suffer with him. They knew that if they denied him they must accept judgement, but they were not at first much concerned with those who had not yet accepted or refused his challenge. The *Revelation of St John* in the New Testament is almost entirely concerned with God's judgement on Israel, the Church and the world. There is little in it that can refer to a particular judgement after death, although it is implied that sinners will be judged, and that those who are rejected will be cast into the lake of fire, the second death. The image is of Gehenna, the Lord's bonfire, where everything that is of no use is finally burnt. This fire is not quenched, and the worm in the refuse does not die, but these images are of destruction, not of torment.

The Apocalypse of St Peter

In the third quarter of the second century this was as well known as the *Revelation of St John*, and it continued to be read as part of the New Testament in some places until the fifth century. The Greek text is no longer extant, but a number of fragments survive, as does an Ethiopian version sufficiently reliable to give us a good idea of the nature of the original. The author was clearly anxious that Christians should have a chance to see the destiny of the dead, good and bad, as they now are in another world. He saw the good with bodies whiter than snow and redder than any rose, the red and white so well combined that their beauty could not be described. Their hair was bright and curly, and lay on their heads and shoulders like wreaths of all sorts of flowers, or a rainbow in the sky. (This is the first hint of haloes on the heads of saints.) Everything around them was bright with light, for the air in their country was like sunshine, smelling of spices and perfumes and fresh fruit. All were equal in glory, and praised God in harmony, each in his own place and part.

In the vision of judgement a particular passage throws light on the nature of the imagery. The seer was taken to a pit or ditch where women stood up to their necks in a mess of dirt with blood in it. In front of them on the bank lay babies squirming and crying. Sparks of fire from their faces struck their mothers in the eyes. These were rejected children, exposed or drowned. We are told that they are given over to an angel for their education, that they may grow into mature persons, but the mothers who would not nurse them are devoured by little carnivorous beasts that come out of the congealed milk in their breasts. The punishment is made to fit the crime, but it must be a mental one. The children are not there, but elsewhere, and the beasts are equally imaginary and equally real. The Ethiopian translator makes the children stand 'in a place of delight', but they are still 'sighing and

crying to God because of their parents'. Origen, the great
Alexandrian scholar of the third century, is nearer to the idea
of the original when he quotes *Isaiah* 50. 11: 'Walk by the light
of your fire and by the brands which you have kindled', in his
First Principles (Bk 2, ch. 10), and goes on to say that 'as in the
body an abundance of eatables or food that disagrees with us'
gives rise to diseases of different kinds, so when the soul has
collected 'an abundance of sins, at the requisite time the
whole mass of evil boils up into punishment'. Then 'con-
science will see exposed before its eyes a kind of history of its
evil deeds, of every foul and disgraceful act, and all unholy
conduct'. We shall meet this idea again in other visions of the
life after death.

The case of the cruel mothers is also important as linking
judgement with concern for the innocent. Perhaps the earliest
absolutely clear case of Christian prayer for the dead is in the
Passion of St Perpetua (203), who saw in a vision her little
brother Dinocrates. He had died of ulcers in the face, a very
painful disease, and she saw him first as the same miserable
little boy, trying to reach a fountain that was far too high for
him. But in another vision, after she had prayed for him, she
saw him drinking from the same fountain, which was now at
the level of his waist, and running away safe and happy. It is
obvious that the fountain is a figure of Christian baptism. By
his sister's prayers Dinocrates was able to receive the benefits
of this world in the other. In St Augustine's time the story
was used as an argument against his doctrine that unbaptised
babies must be in hell. He replied first that there was no
evidence that Dinocrates had not been baptised, and secondly
that in any case he was old enough to know right from wrong.
He allowed for the possibility of a holy pagan, but could not
see any innate morality in an untrained baby. Their suffering
in hell might be reduced to a minimum, but they could not
grow up into salvation. This teaching established a clear distinction between purgatory and hell in western Christendom.

This distinction never obtained in the east, where judgement
scenes are relatively rare. There is one in the refectory of the
Great Lavra on Mount Athos, and one ascribed to Byzantine
artists of about 1100 on the west wall of the cathedral at
Torcello, an island close to Venice. In this mosaic the symbolic
nature of the imagery should be obvious. The souls indeed are
weighed at the last trump, and the damned on the left have
their feet licked by fire. But one of them sits enthroned on a
figure of Death or Hades, in a place evidently fashioned after
the model of Abraham's bosom. (It has been suggested that he
is anti-Christ.) Of those who have gone farther down into the
inferno some burn and one stands in ice, but four are merely
naked, looking this way or that. The heads below them are
burning or being eaten by worms, but they themselves are as
they were in this world, except that they wear nothing. On the
other side are a group of innocent children, standing under a
tree of life and looking anxiously up at a stern but benevolent
saint. In the next compartment on the same level St John the
Baptist and St Peter stand beside what looks like an open
coffin, upright and guarded by a cherub. It is clear from other

The Adoration of the Magi. One of the leaves
of the *Très Riches Heures du Duc de Berry*
painted by the Limbourg brothers in the early
fifteenth century.

examples that this is the door leading by a stair to the higher
levels where saints are praying and praising God. In the
whole composition hell, though fairly populous, takes up less
than a quarter of the space, and this is in itself in contrast with
the general run of western dooms.

Gates and bridges

The hymns of St Ephrem, originally written in Syriac in the
fourth century and widely translated into Greek and Slavonic,
are full of vivid descriptions of the heavenly life and of the
antechamber to the heavenly places where souls are left who
sin without full responsibility for their decisions. His sermon
on the last judgement is one of the sources for an anonymous
Russian sermon *On the celestial powers*, sometimes ascribed to
St Abraham of Smolensk in the twelfth century. Another is the
visions of Theodora in the life of St Basil the Younger. In

THE VISION OF EZEKIEL

these her soul is escorted by two angels through a number of
gates. At each of these she is required to give her own account
of her offences, at the first of slanders, whether spoken aloud
or kept to herself, to a guardian of the gate who knows all the
circumstances and all the answers. He cannot be deceived but
he can understand faults and failings a great deal better than
the penitent sinner.

The image is evidently taken from the ordeal of passing
through the customs at Constantinople. Bishop Liutprand of
Cremona was held up for three weeks on his way out in 968,
not long after Theodora's death, on the suspicion that he
might be taking imperial purple silk to the rival Roman
emperor, Otto the Great. He complained bitterly that all his
baggage was searched and his garments thrown about in dis-
array, and that no one would accept a bribe to stop. No
doubt the customs were an important source of revenue,
but the risk in going through was the exposure of the real truth
about your baggage, of the possible presence for instance of a
particular kind of soap that was believed to possess some
perilous qualities, and might not be introduced, under a heavy
penalty, into any house in the city.

In Theodora's visions the road from gate to gate is pre-

Ezekiel's vision of the resurrection in *Ezekiel* 37,
as represented in the synagogue at Dura-
Europos, copied on the site and completed in
Newhaven by an American artist, Herbert J.
Gute. Yale University Art Gallery.
Above right:
In this stained-glass window, sentimental as it
is, we can see the concern for infant innocence
that appears in the *Apocalypse of St Peter* and
in the Assumptions of El Greco and Rubens.
The children on the ground are sprouting
wings, but they are very human, and the angel
on the left may be keeping an eye on them.
Nineteenth century, Bourges Cathedral.

cipitously steep. If the soul passed all the tests he or she had still to cross a perilous bridge overhanging hell before reaching the vestibule of paradise. The bridge, but not the gates, appears in a story told to St Gregory the Great during his stay in Constantinople around 580. This is one of a number of stories told in his *Dialogues* about those who nearly died, or did in fact die but returned to tell the tale. One stood on the bridge of dread, seeing the happy land and its many mansions on the other side, but horrible fumes arose from below, and a friend of his and of St Gregory who put his foot down over the edge became the object of an exciting battle between angels above and devils below. The struggle was interrupted only by his own return to the body. Before this he had seen among the sufferers a high ecclesiastic who, as everyone knew, inflicted punishment for the pleasure of doing so, and not in reluctant obedience. It is interesting to note that the object of the struggle on the bridge was still alive and profited by his friend's precognition.

St Gregory, who was pope from 590 to 604, believed that more information was becoming available about the state of the departed as the dawn of the last day broke. He cites the case of the holy deacon Paschasius, whose dalmatic (vestment) had

The Good Shepherd in a mosaic in the oratory of Galla Placidia, built by her towards the middle of the fifth century at Ravenna.

healed a demoniac. Nevertheless he was surprised after his death by Bishop Germanus of Capua, who saw him standing under the hot water in the baths of St Angelo, whither the bishop had been directed by his physicians for a bodily complaint, probably rheumatic. Asked why he was there, Paschasius complained that he suffered thus for supporting, in good faith, the wrong pope. The bishop went away to pray about it and came back to find him no longer there. Less edifying to our ears is the tale of Deusdedit, who saw his heavenly mansion being built, but only on Sundays, when he went to church and dispensed charities. He made shoes during the week, but this did not help.

These stories did much to develop and standardise views on this subject in the Latin west, where St Gregory's *Dialogues* and letters had a wide circulation. Popular notions in the Christian east were rather different. They may be seen in the *Apocalypse of St Paul*, probably put into its present form towards the end of the fourth century, and in the later *Apocalypse of the Virgin*. Both are merciful to souls in hell. St Paul wins for all of them a respite at the weekend. The Virgin pleads for Christians only and gets them a summer holiday from Easter to Whitsunday.

The problem of late repentance

The Venerable Bede gives us two visions, both on the authority of informants known to him. One is from the life of Fursa

or Fursey, an Irish missionary in East Anglia. As he was
carried by angels towards heaven he was told to look down and
saw the fires that would consume the world – falsehood,
cupidity, dissension or debate, and pitiless cruelty. These
combined into one huge flame and came after him. He saw the
demons in the fire, but with the help of the angels he passed
through it once unscathed, and saw the saints. On his way
back into the body a soul was thrown at him whose garment
he had taken, by way of payment at a deathbed 'for the sake of
saving the other's soul'. His cheek was scorched, and his
guardian angel told him: 'If you had not taken the goods of
this man dead in his sins, his pains would not burn in you.'
This was the prelude to 'wholesome discourse on what is to be
done with those who repent at the hour of death'. The same
difficult subject is prominent in the vision of Drythelm, a
Northumbrian householder with a wife and family, who in
consequence of his experiences left them and became an
anchorite in the Abbey of Melrose. This follows a pattern
which recurs fairly often in later visions, perhaps because
Bede was widely read. It may be however that Drythelm was
helped at Melrose to put his visions into a standard form
which may be of Irish origin.

He was taken by his angelic guide in a north-easterly
direction into a broad and deep valley with fire on one side
and ice on the other. This is not hell, but leads to the edge

of the pit. The late repentant, tossed to and fro between fire and ice, may get so near that at any rate they fear falling into it. Drythelm himself was alone on the edge for some agonising moments. Rescued, he was taken south and east to a long and high wall. Somehow or other he and his guide mounted to the top, where he found a broad and pleasant field. This is not heaven, but leads to it. This could be called a fourfold division, but it is more threefold than fourfold. Those on the top of the wall are certain of their salvation; it is the lot of most of us to be tossed from fire to ice at hell's edge.

The problem of late repentance had important effects on religious practice in the Middle Ages. In the time of St Augustine mass in commemoration of any deceased Christian looked much the same. He had to insist that it was a thanksgiving for the good and a propitiatory offering for those who were not so bad, but of little or no use to the really wicked. But as liturgical prayers were more precisely regulated, distinctions emerged between masses in commemoration of saints, of others in good standing, and of those under penitential discipline. Forms in aid of these last came into common use for those reconciled to the Church on their deathbeds, or cut off by circumstances from any chance of penitence or reconciliation. The theory was that they had repented at the last, or no mass could be said for them, but in a great number of cases warriors and other slain in the tumults of the time had to be given the benefit of the doubt. In such circumstances, in the eyes of their friends, prayer and the propitiatory effect of the sacrifice of the mass were even more important. It came to be thought that the mass for penitents was more efficacious than a mass of thanksgiving for those in good standing. Finally from a mixture of humility and anxiety everyone wanted one for himself and his loved ones. This was generally repeated at regular intervals on the third, seventh and thirtieth days after death, and at anniversaries afterwards. Later it came to be believed that thirty masses on consecutive days was specially effective. In monasteries this could be supplemented by the Office for the Dead for brethren and benefactors.

In the first half of the eleventh century the feast of the dead at the beginning of November began to be divided between All Saints on the first and All Souls on the second of the month. This feast is itself of Irish origin, connected with the ancient festival of Samhain, where cattle were sacrificed before the winter. All Saints retained this aspect of a feast in honour of saints and heroes, but on All Souls the mass and office had a penitential aspect, in commemoration of the faithful and not so faithful departed. A traveller from Aquitaine who was a frequent visitor at the great monastery of Cluny, met on one of the Greek islands or (in another version in the Sahara) an anchorite with an intimate knowledge of the demonic world.

The anchorite told him of the wrath of the demons 'whom I have often heard lamenting and making no small complaint, because by the prayers of monks and by alms for the poor . . . again and again through the mercy of God the souls of the damned are freed from their pains'. He wished the monks of Cluny to know that specially great complaints were made

This ivory plaque shows the seated figures of death and hell on the right, and the children on the lap of a saint on the left. The throne in the centre is prepared for Christ's coming. The dead rise to the last trump on the right. Byzantine work of the eleventh or twelfth century. Victoria and Albert Museum.
Right:
The voyage of St Brendan. His ship is sustained by a sea-monster in this illustration from MS Pal. Germ. 60 in the University Library at Heidelberg, Germany.

against them and their abbot, 'whereby they may the more persist in prayers and alms for those in pain, that joy may be multiplied in heaven and grief and loss inflicted on the devil'. Raoul Glaber, who was the first to report this, makes him say: 'So much power has the constant offering of the life-giving sacrifice, that hardly a day passes in which this business does not rescue souls from the power of malignant demons'. Raoul reports that at Cluny such masses were celebrated continuously 'from the first dawn of day until lunchtime, on account of the number of brethern'.

St Patrick's Purgatory

The story of St Brandon or St Brendan, in Irish Latin about an Irish saint, probably dates from the ninth century, perhaps earlier. This is evidence that in the Irish tradition the island of the blessed – separated into accessible and inaccessible portions as in Drythelm's vision – and the mouth of hell are in the Atlantic. The latter is a volcano, probably suggested by those in Iceland. St Brandon on his voyage did not venture to land in the neighbourhood, though he lost a monk there. He met on a nearby rock, washed by the waves, Judas Iscariot, who explained that his ordinary torment was to burn like a lump of lead in a crucible, day and night, at the bottom of the crater, but he had a holiday in the sea not only at weekends, from the first to the second vespers of every Sunday, but from Christmas to the Epiphany, from Easter to Whitsun, and on two festivals of the Virgin. There is evidence that some form of the *Apocalypse of the Virgin* was known in Ireland, and it is possible that this measure of relief was derived from this and from the *Apocalypse of St Paul*.

A series of stories relating to an island in Lough Derg, in County Donegal, begins with the descent of Owain, a knight with a Welsh name in the retinue of King Stephen, recorded by Henry of Saltrey as taking place in 1153. As this is not very interesting, and the account of it reached Henry at second hand, it may be better to begin with a comparatively sober statement in the *Topography of Ireland* by Gerald of Wales (1196), who says that the island is divided into two parts. One contains a church frequently visited by saints and angels. The other is covered with rugged crags and inhabited entirely by devils. It contains not one but nine pits, and if anyone ventures to spend the night in one of them, he is severely tormented, but 'it is said that anyone who has once submitted to these torments as a penance imposed upon him, will not afterwards undergo the pains of hell, unless he commit some sin of a deeper dye'.

Owain and others were supposed to have obtained permission from their own bishop, and from the prior of the monastery on the island, to make the perilous attempt. After mass and communion they were taken in procession to the door of a cave and locked in. If they were there in the morning, all was well. They might be expected to undergo further pentitential exercises, reflecting on their experiences, but it was to be presumed that these had been for their profit. If they were not discovered, it was supposed that the devils had caught them and kept them. Froissart tells of a conversation he had with Sir William Lisle, who had passed the night there with a companion. They had gone down as though into a cellar, and met with hot vapour, but this put them to sleep. They dreamt unusual dreams, but could not remember them.

William of Stranton, who came from Durham and went down into the cave on the Friday after Holy Cross Day 14 September 1409, has an interesting story. The Prior gave him a prayer to say if troubled by any spirit, good or evil, and after a short time, like Sir William Lisle, he fell asleep. In his dream he saw two north-country saints, St John of Bridlington and his sister St Ive, who introduced themselves and gave him directions. They came to his rescue on other occasions, most notably when he met 'a sister of mine, that was dead long-to-fore in a pestilence time, and another man which I knew welle that my sister loved wel whiles they

The weighing of souls on a painted funerary casket from Egypt. Anubis holds the scales, while Thoth, the scribe of the gods, records the results. This weighing of souls appears on many Christian dooms. Twenty-sixth dynasty.

lived in this world'. His sister accused him of stopping her marriage with her lover by saying that 'we should nothir have joye of other, and for that cause we lefte hit', but 'this man standing here loved me, and I loved him'. If William had not interfered, they would have brought three souls to God, presumably their children.

St John of Bridlington, who came to William's aid, implied in his reproach that some question of social status was involved, for he insisted that any one who comes between a man and a woman, 'if the man be of never so high kin, or the woman of never so low kin, if they love one another, sins in holy Church against God and his Christendom in deed', and shall have much tribulation. The rest of William's story is sincere but not so interesting. Those who swore by God's members, by his eyes or his wounds, had their own torn out and soldered back again. Proud bishops were tormented by their proud servants and by serpents, toads and snakes that came out of the ornamental edges of their robes. What William remembered most plainly was his sister saying: 'This

This church and its surrounding plant was completed in 1929, and the island extended on concrete piers to make room for it. Here pilgrims still come in large numbers between Whitsunday and August 15th, the feast of the Assumption, fasting for three days on one meal a day of toast and tea, and watching for a day and a night without sleep. They make a round of stations, some of them involving walking with bare feet over sharp stones. These can be seen in the centre of the picture between the tree and the obelisk. As they put on their shoes to go home they say 'never again'. This is part of the rite which was once believed to complete their purgation, but in modern times of easy travel quite a number of regulars come every year. The island is in Lough Derg, but as no underground cave is included in the stations, we may suppose that it is not the original island to which pilgrimages were made from the twelfth to the fifteenth century, but the other which became a centre of resistance to the English government in the sixteenth and seventeenth centuries.

This western judgement scene bears some resemblance to eastern forms, for instance in the treatment of innocent children on the left at the bottom, and in the open door with the redeemed passing in, but the condemned take up more space and are treated with much greater ferocity. It is on the tympanum of the west front of the Abbey church of Conques in Languedoc, of the eleventh century.

man standing here loved me, and I loved him.'

St Patrick's Purgatory was closed by the order of Pope Alexander VI in 1497, on the complaint of a monk from Holland, who thought it was a fraud. But before long the Irish discovered another entry on a smaller island, more remote from the shore. The resort of Irish Catholics there caused concern to the government at various times in the seventeenth and eighteenth centuries, and also excited ridicule from Protestants. But Calderon wrote a play about it. Among the apologies for it was one that identified Ulster with the place where Ulysses descended into the lower world. If the situation of heaven became less definite with the switch from Ptolemaic to Copernican astronomy the interior of the earth was still known to be hot, and the infernal regions had their exits and entrances through volcanoes. The common teaching continued to develop in precision as mythology was translated into the language of geography. This geography of purgatory no doubt owes much to older notions of a fairy land under the earth or beyond the sea and the sky, but in the Middle

Ages it was not always set in a place. There is a good story of
a piece of ice that was given by some fisherfolk to their gouty
bishop, who as he sat with his feet on it heard a soul demand-
ing the regular sequence of thirty masses to get him out. A
number of interruptions impeded this, but the bishop decided
that these were contrived by devils, and resolved to concen-
trate until the ice melted and the soul escaped. Here we have a
material, ice, that may be anywhere, but souls may still be
tossed between this ice and fire under the earth, as Judas in
The Voyage of St Brendan spent part of the time being cooked
and part of the time being washed by the cold Atlantic.

Eastern and western views
In controversies between East and West in the Middle Ages
the Greeks were often accused by the Latins of not believing in
purgatorial pains and penalties, but in plans for reunion at
Lyons in 1274 and at Ferrara and Florence in 1438–9 the
point was not pressed. Both sides believed that penitent souls
are purged by cathartic and purifying pains. They agreed in

Joachim and Anna fondling their small daughter at Kahrie Cami (formerly the church of St Mary in Chora), where this fresco was made in 1305 or 1320, in Constantinople.
Right:
The Flavian Amphitheatre in Rome, more commonly called the Colosseum. Built during the reign of the just emperor Titus, it became the scene of martyrdom under later emperors.

praying for the dead, but the Greeks were prepared to pray for a wider class of sinners, nor did they think material fires could hurt disembodied souls. As we have seen, in popular Greek mythology the souls in hell are not cut off entirely from God's mercy. One of their great theologians, Mark of Ephesus, argued at Florence that the references to material fire in the Scriptures should all be interpreted as a fire beginning after the day of judgement. Purgatory is not a place where souls give satisfaction to the divine justice, but the spiritual fire in which they are being refined.

Dante, who wrote when these controversies were at their height, followed the Irish tradition in that he put the mountain leading to the earthly paradise far away in the western ocean, but his purgatory is on the way to paradise, rather than at the entrance to hell. He went through hell to find it, but out by a back stair to the southern hemisphere. In his poem the fire is spiritual, and in purgatory lovable. This links him with the older tradition perhaps communicated to him by the basilicas at Ravenna, where he spent much of his life in exile. His ideal Christian emperor is Justinian, not Charlemagne. He followed the Western tradition in making Virgil return to his place in limbo, in the highest regions of hell, but it is significant that the poet travelled with him through purgatory to the entrance of the earthly paradise. In the east he would have been with Plato in heaven.

The important difference is not between east and west but between Dante and St Patrick's Purgatory. Those who went to Lough Derg were making a deliberate venture into a dangerous terrain, like speleologists taking a medium with them to hold a seance underground. Dante's poem is a highly conscious construction, but no one who is sensitive to the process of poetic creation will doubt that it has a basis in an experience of communication. In this he believed Virgil and Beatrice, perhaps some others, to be involved. There is nothing alien to the Christian tradition in such collaboration between the dead and the living, but it is myth, enigma or prophecy. It is not intended to be taken literally, and when it occurs today, as I think it sometimes does, we should be careful in interpreting it to remember that the timescale is different from ours.

The necessity of mythology

Our need of myth is seen most clearly in the face of death, for few can be sure of extinction, and in this matter complete agnosticism is necessarily unsatisfying. Whitehead, who among modern philosophers devoted most thought to the subject, spoke of objective immortality, by which he meant that in some way the sum of our lives is conserved in a mind that includes them all. This could be developed into a modern vision of judgement, but for this it would need some elaboration, some myth that such conservation is done through an icon recording dominant motives and key events, like the group of icons commemorating episodes in the lives of Eastern saints, or through a biographical film with key episodes.

Christ enthroned on the round world between angels in a mosaic of the sixth century at St Vitale, Ravenna.
Left:
Christ as judge trampling on sin, with St Peter standing on his right and St Paul on his left. Sarcophagus of Junius Bassus (A.D. 359). The Vatican, Rome.

These would account for apparitions, including ghosts.

I have even thought that some experiences which have been taken to support the transmigration of souls might be better explained, not as residual memories of a former life, but as the impact of someone in an earlier generation at critical moments of our own development. To take an instance, the communication of music by dead composers could be interpreted as telepathy with them in their unfinished or forgotten work, and need not imply that they continue indefinitely to produce music in a like style. If the style were different, this might be regarded as evidence of some distortion through the receiving agent, or as an argument against the authenticity of the communication. We should hardly regard it as evidence of development after death. We may meet with some experience that comes to us with overwhelming force as a sign of change and growth in the life after death, but the only part of this that can be shown to others is a change in us. In this sense the search for proofs of survival is a wild-goose chase.

Our difficulty in the use of traditional Christian myth has

124

Christ with the seven gifts of the Holy Spirit,
interestingly represented as birds of different
kinds, in a window of the thirteenth century in
Le Mans Cathedral.

more to do with time and less with space than is commonly
thought. I do not believe that heaven above and the under-
world below were taken topographically when myths were
entertained as mythology. The three-storied universe was
indeed taken as a map by Cosmas Indicopleustes, a Syrian
mariner of the sixth century, but he was exceptionally zealous
for the historical interpretation of the Bible. As we have seen,
hell and purgatory were very diversely placed in the Middle
Ages, and saints and angels were in action everywhere. But
Christians generally did insist that a general resurrection must
take place on earth at some time in the future. As we have
seen, particular judgement after death became more important
as time went on. Those who have passed the celestial toll-
gates, or climbed the mountain of purgatory, are counted as
saved already, and have their part in the kingdom, if not
immediately, but the day of judgement remains the climax of
the story. It is this that needs interpretation if death is to be
regarded rather as a change in the manner of our existence in
the body than as a provisional interruption of it.

The early Christians accepted the idea of an immortal,

The Christ of *Revelation* 1. 12–16: 'In the
midst of seven golden lamp-stands, one like a
son of man . . . In his right hand (here his left)
he held seven stars, from his mouth issued a
sharp two-edged sword, and his face was like
the sun shining in full strength'. From a window of the early thirteenth century at Bourges
Cathedral.

incorporeal spirit from the philosophy of the world around
them. Our psychology makes us so aware of interaction
between soul and body that the life of an incorporeal spirit
may seem as shadowy as that of a shade in Sheol, but the
resurrection could be conceived as access to other bodies in
some fashion beyond our present understanding, of which
telepathy may give us an inkling. Despite the insistence of
some zealots on the literal sense of Scripture, I should be
inclined to read the fantastic figures of sea-monsters and lions
regurgitating their victims, so often found in representations
of the last judgement, as evidence of an understanding of the
resurrection of the body that would stress the difference
between this and mere immortality, and yet recognise the
paradoxical character of any description. It is significant that
denial of 'the Resurrection of the same numerical particles'
was condemned at Oxford in 1690, at the threshold of the age
of reason. This is not a survival of medieval obscurantism, but
a symptom of the decay of the poetic imagination in an age
when everything must be understood as true or false by the
same standards of evidence.

126

Death and resurrection are only part of a larger problem. In the view that has come to prevail in India and other parts of the Far East, human souls are part of a larger class of spirits fallen into a world of illusion, who just find their way out again. Creation and the fall interlock, because the material world in which we appear to live is an illusion created by our desires. We in the west are more disposed to believe that this is the real world and our proper place. In the Christian view it is God's creation, and man is his chosen race, intended from his first beginnings to control this planet at any rate, if not the moon and other planets as well. His fall is not a cause but a consequence of existence in freedom. There is no direct contradiction between this and the biological view of evolution through natural selection. Both imply a linear view of progress in history, and in this sense stand together against any theory that sees in terrestrial life no more than the continued repetition of a celestial theme. But in a great deal of our thinking about evolution there is an unacknowledged confusion between scientific hypotheses about genetics, mutations and the origin of species, and an evolutionary view of the progress of life from the slime on the beaches to man and perhaps beyond, which has imaginative appeal, but nothing like scientific proof. This kind of myth demands an end as well as an origin for the story of man. It therefore becomes a myth of inevitable progress which may break down under the strain of interpreting what is ambiguous in the signs of the times, and become a myth of crisis and disaster, as in the more sinister novels of H. G. Wells and some recent science fiction.

There may well be a real affinity between the insight that gives rise to myths and the creative vision that sees scientific hypotheses, but neither of these should be confused with the painful process whereby hypotheses are scientifically verified. The difference can be seen most plainly in the case of history, which is always mythologised to some degree, because the facts presented without selection are not in themselves interesting. A great deal of historical research consists in undermining the myths, in demythologising history by showing that the Tory party in the time of the younger Pitt were not the direct heirs of the Cavaliers, or the Whigs of the Roundheads, that the facts are more complicated, as they always are. In such enquiries the most interesting result may not be the complex truth, so hard to state with full justice to all involved, but the motives of the myth and the history of its development.

On the problem of Christian origins we have a collection of materials in St Paul's letters, of which five are almost unchallenged by scholars, while the others are less certainly his, but certainly letters, and early letters, like those of St John. The modern 'quest for historical Jesus' has turned to a great extent to the relations of these letters with the Gospels. It has a background in earlier controversy before the question of the history in the Gospels began to be debated. As collections of texts to support a theological argument the Epistles, or parts of St Paul's, were more useful than the Gospels in the scholastic disputes of the Middle Ages. The theology of the Protestant Reformation was largely constructed round them,

Christ between the symbols of the four evangelists in the wooden stave church of about 1250 at Torpo in Norway.

and much Roman Catholic theology around replies to this on the questions concerning man in the state of innocence, the fall, and grace. At times this had led to reactions where Jesus and Paul were opposed, but on the whole the current of scholarship has flowed towards an interpretation of the Gospels in the light of the Epistles as primarily a summons to confident faith in God. A recent form of this interpretation is to read them as quasi-mythical presentations of the Church's first response to the fact of Jesus, which could be translated, with St Paul's assistance, into existentialist terms. That may be worth doing for those of us who are existentialists, but is it more than a movement from myth to myth?

The quest for the historical Jesus must still go on and remains important for any one who takes history seriously, not only because of the demand for evidence in our own day, but because in the nature of the case the Christian proclamation is and has always been about what happened on and after Calvary. Nevertheless the understanding of myth is not only part of the way to recover the history, but important in itself because myths are evidence not only of how people thought, but of how they actually think. As we have seen, the Christian hope of a happy end for the history of the world, of what we call progress, arose in the first place from confidence in the resurrection of Christ. The first Christians made no sharp division between his resurrection, bringing the captives from Sheol, and the general resurrection still to come. These fell apart as the last judgement was postponed to a distant future, but tended to come together again as the decisive moments in the judgement upon individual souls were associated with the passage to a new condition of life at the time of our death.

Our present knowledge of the vast extent of the time span of human prehistory and history, of the multiplicity of the generation of men and women, makes it more difficult for us to conceive of the day of doom as a final climax where all these judgements meet in terms of space and time. But it may be that the dead are growing nearer to one another and to us, and that as we become more aware of all our ancestors, pagan as well as Christian, of saints of other religions or none, and of those who died with little or no belief in a life after death, working their passage to clarity and wholeness in and through us, the resurrection of the body may acquire a new meaning, for Christians in terms of participation in the risen life of Christ. A Romanian theologian has lately written: 'The light and power of Christ's Resurrection invest and penetrate everything.' He goes on to insist that 'each of us will rise simply as a member of humanity' and that what makes the Church truly catholic is her sense of the world's solidarity in Christ and of her own duty to work for the deepening of this solidarity. This leaves the door wide open to other ways of conceiving our universal human participation in the new man. What is objectively certain is not the image but the presence, more personal than all of us, but penetrating all things—not the myth but the life that all myths reflect, the Spirit proceeding from the source that Christians call the Father through the Word whom they worship as the Christ, the Son of the living God.

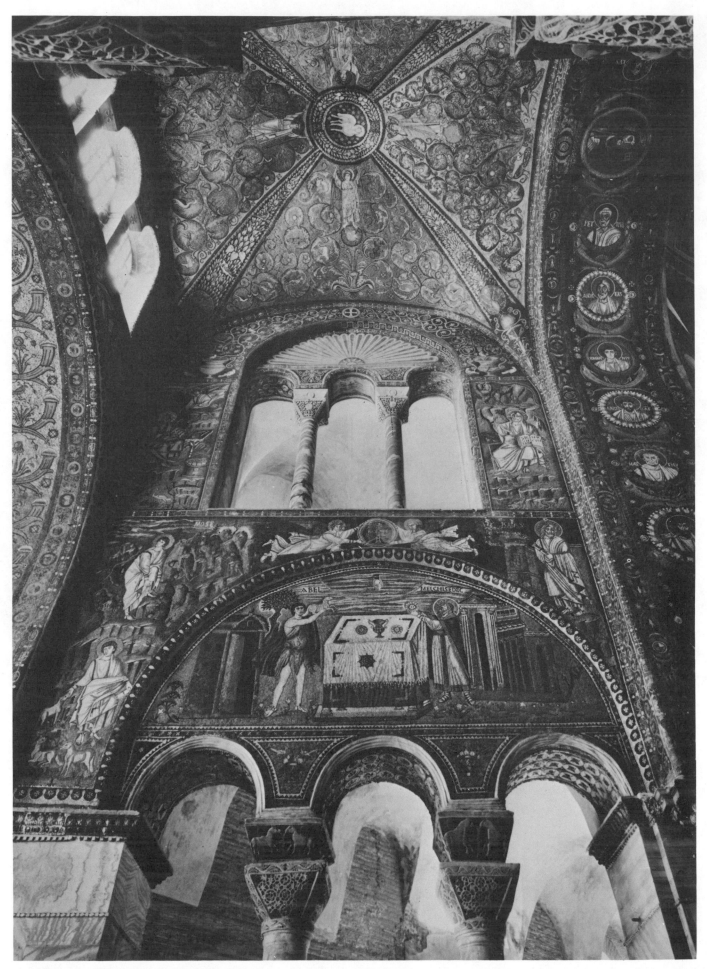

The materials

Most social anthropologists are hostile to general theories of religious origins. The reasons for this are well stated by Professor Evans-Pritchard in his lectures on *Theories of Primitive Religion*, delivered at Aberystwyth in 1962. Claude Lévi-Strauss, whose books are now being translated from French into English, is more concerned with the structure of religions than with their origins. I have learned much from *The Savage Mind* and from a chapter on the study of myth in *Structural Anthropology*. Lévi-Strauss is sometimes regarded as a successor of those who interpret religion entirely in terms of sociology, as Durkheim did at the beginning of this century, but this view seems to me a mistake. He regards myth and

The sarcophagus of Adelphia. On the left at the top a redeemed soul is being introduced to the saints. On the right is the scene of the nativity. In the second row Adelphia and her husband Valerius are together flanked by Moses striking the rock, the sacrifice of Isaac and a number of Christ's miracles, e.g. on the right the healing of the man born blind, the multiplication of the loaves and fishes, and the raising of Lazarus from the dead. Below on the left are the three young men refusing to worship the golden image, as in *Daniel* 3, in the centre the visit of the wise men to the Virgin and her child, on the right the fall of man and Christ's entry in Jerusalem. It is a mistake to look for a consistent scheme of symbolism, but the narrative style is evident. Marble, carved in the fourth century, at Syracuse.
Left:
The sacrifices of Abel and Melchizedek in a mosaic of the sixth century at St Vitale, Ravenna.

ritual as the expression of the relationship between a society and its whole environment, and not simply of relations within the society.

Mircea Eliade is a Romanian, who made his reputation as an authority on Siberian shamanism, though his book on the subject was not translated into English until 1964. Social and political pressures drove him from Bucharest to Paris and then to Chicago, where he became associated with the group founded by Joachim Wach and concerned with the history of religions. His books include *Myths, Dreams and Mysteries, Myth and Reality,* and *The Myth of the Eternal Return.* The new year festival in Babylon is well described by Henri Frankfort in *Kingship and the Gods* (1948). This includes illustrations of Egyptian art, including one of the sun's boats passing beneath the heavenly cow, which throw light on the Egyptian capacity to hold incompatible ideas together.

Before the Bible by Cyrus H. Gordon is valuable as a bridge between Homer and the Patriarchal narratives in Genesis. Stuart Piggot in *Prehistoric India* (1950) and more recently F. R. and Bridgett Allchin in *The Birth of Indian Civilisation* (1968) have shown how much history there is in the Rig-Veda, but to see what was done with it we need to consult Ninian

Smart's *Doctrine and Argument in Indian Philosophy*, and Edward Conze on *Buddhist Thought in India* or his shorter book on *Buddhism*.

The Earliest Lives of Jesus by R. H. Grant is useful in putting the Gospels and their first interpreters into their setting in Greek literature and criticism. To this I owe my reference to Origen's defence of the virgin birth of Christ, found on pp. 28–36 of Professor Henry Chadwick's translation of Origen's work against Celsus (*c.* 248). The early Roman baptismal questions are in *The Apostolic Tradition of Hippolytus* (*c.* 217), of which the latest English edition is by Dom Gregory Dix, corrected by Professor Henry Chadwick. Accounts of changing attitudes to mystical interpretation can be found in a volume of essays on *The Church's Use of the Bible*, edited by Professor Denis Nineham, and in the second volume of *The Cambridge History of the Bible*. Of the change in attitudes to history a good account is in *British Antiquity* by T. D. Kendrick, and from a rather different standpoint by David Douglas in *English Scholars, 1660–1730*.

In the crisis of Biblical criticism in the nineteenth century the important differences between England and Germany were largely due to a group of Anglican scholars who had read more of the Christian Fathers than most Protestants, and more of the Greek Fathers than all but a few Roman Catholics. The Greek *Philokalia*, an important collection mainly of mystical writing, was prepared at Corinth and Mount Athos, and published in Venice in 1782–3. It was later expanded in Russian and abbreviated in French and English translations. But Greek influence in England goes back to the seventeenth century, when Richard Montague was at work on Photius, Ussher and Pearson on St Ignatius, and William Beveridge on the Byzantine canonists, while John Ernst Grabë, a Prussian refugee in Oxford, published an edition of St Irenaeus and collections of earlier materials.

Creation, flood and fall

The debate about myth and ritual is summarised in a symposium, *Myth, Ritual and Kingship*, edited by S. H. Hooke in 1958. It arose in part out of earlier symposia also edited by Hooke, *Myth and Ritual* in 1933 and *The Labyrinth* in 1935, but an important part was played by Swedish scholars, notably Ivor Engnell, whose *Studies in Divine Kingship in the Ancient Near East* came out in a second edition in 1967, and by Aubrey R. Johnson, whose contribution to *The Labyrinth* on the place of the king in the ritual of the Temple at Jerusalem was followed by a number of monographs including *Sacral Kingship in early Israel*. The whole school were attacked by Henri Frankfort in an epilogue to *Kingship and the Gods*. Most commentators on Genesis tend to ignore their work and to exaggerate the difference between Jewish history and Gentile myth.

The translations of Christian prayers are my own, reused by leave of the Faith Press from *Basic Liturgy*, published by them in 1961. The Latin of the one from the Abbey of Reichenau can be found in an edition of the *Missale Gallicanum Vetus* by L. H. Mohlberg and others. The Spanish prayer is in the

Fishes on either side of a basket of loaves in a pavement originally belonging to the church of the multiplication of the loaves and fishes, made in the middle of the fifth century by the shores of the sea of Galilee, where it still is, close to the main road between Tiberias and Capernaum.
Right:
A miracle of the true cross from the *Historia Sanctae Crucis* of 1483. Royal Library, Brussels.

Hier heeft helena dat cruys ons Heren
In tween ghedeylt tot goods eren
Dat een stuc heeft si tot iherusalem ghelaten
Dat ander stuc nam se mede hore straten

Mozarabic *Missale Mixtum* for the Sunday after the octave of the Epiphany, but I found it originally in the *Liber Sacramentorum,* a manuscript of the tenth century edited by Dom Marius Férotin. There it is the first of the 'quotidian' of ordinary masses, probably older than the rest. The prayers in book seven of the compilation called *The Apostolic Constitutions* have been the subject of much learned debate. The view here owes much to a book by Erwin R. Goodenough, *By light, light,* to which I was introduced by Père Bouyer of the Oratory, but my references to Philo have been found with the help of F. R. Tennant's book on *The Sources of the Doctrine of the Fall and of Original Sin.* Most of them are from the *De Mundi Opificio,* a commentary on the opening chapters of Genesis which is put first in collections of his works. *The Book of the Secrets of Enoch* was translated from the Slavonic by W. R. Morfull, and edited with an introduction by R. H. Charles for the Oxford press in 1898. Its relation to Alexandrian Judaism is discussed in F. R. Tennant's book.

I first became interested in the state of innocence in Eden as a mythical model for human perfection through reading in Père de Lubac's *Surnaturel* (1946) of the debate between Jesuit theologians and their critics on 'the state of pure nature' between 1560 and 1640. This book is not easily accessible, but the same debate is summarised, not so perceptively, in Nigel Abercrombie's *Origins of Jansenism.*

The views of St Irenaeus are conveniently concentrated in chapters 11–23 of his *Apostolic Preaching.* Those of St Augustine are more widely dispersed but books 13 and 14 of *The City of God* are devoted to Adam and Eve. A comparison between him and St Irenaeus has been made by John Hick in *Freedom and the Love of God.* In a brief but important lecture on *St Augustine and Christian Platonism,* delivered at Villanova in the U.S.A., Hilary Armstrong has compared him with St Gregory of Nyssa, whose views on sex are summarised in *L'image de Dieu chez St Grégoire de Nysse* by Roger Leys, S. J., pp. 106–110.

In the selection from his works in the collection of *Nicene and Post-Nicene Fathers* is an essay on the deaths of infants which contrasts sharply with St Augustine's views on the first book of the *Confessions* and elsewhere. To him the hub of the difficulty lay in the limits of a baby's 'natural delight . . . in gentle rocking that induces and then sweetens slumber. Any happiness beyond this the tenderness of its years . . . prevents it from feeling.' In dying therefore a baby can only partake of the life of God as he does in his mother's, until the time comes when he can receive more 'from that abundant supply of the truly existent which is offered'.

Nothing is said of the problem of unbaptised infants, which so troubled St Augustine that where his influence prevailed infant baptism became a rite normally performed in the first moments of life, and associated with the removal of stains inseparably connected with the conditions of our existence. But as we have seen, earlier Christians were concerned with the afterlife and growth of exposed infants, who had certainly not been baptised.

The two cities

Summaries of Rabbinical views on the evil imagination and on the intercourse of the 'sons of God' with the 'daughters of men' will be found in F. R. Tennant's book and also in Bampton lectures given by N. P. Williams in 1924 on *Ideas of the Fall and Original Sin*. More material of the same kind has been found in a great collection of *Legends of the Jews* made by Louis Ginzberg. Ideas of the origin and destiny of the soul are summarised in the first volume on pp. 55–7, with notes and references in the fifth on pp. 75–8.

The views of St Thomas Aquinas on the use of magical means, such as gazing into crystals, to obtain a weather forecast, were discussed by Fr Victor White, O.P., in *God and the Unconscious*. According to his life, probably by St Athanasius, St Anthony held that the methods used by Egyptian priests to predict the extent of the inundation of the Nile in the coming year depended upon advance information on rainfall in Ethiopia, conveyed demonically, or as we should say by extrasensory perception, which takes no account of time and is often right, but sometimes wrong.

References to Rahab, the Hebrew equivalent of the monster Tiamat, appear from time to time in the Old Testament, for instance in *Psalms* 87.3 and *Isaiah* 51.9. An account of *The Anti-Christ Legend* was produced in 1895 by William Bousset. St Ephrem's sermon, whose authenticity Bousset did not acknowledge, can generally be found in collections of his works. An English paraphrase was published in 1711. In Soloviev's prophecy Pope Peter II and the Elder John are identified with the two witnesses in chapter 11 of the *Revelation of St John* in the New Testament. They fall dead and lie buried for some time before rising again. Meanwhile a friend of the Emperor and AntiChrist has been elected Pope, and Professor Pauli has to lead the opposition, Catholic and Orthodox as well as Protestant, as Barth led the opposition to Hitler from Basle in the 1930s. The visions of St Irenaeus are in his book *Against Heresies* (Book V, ch. 3, section 3).

The place of the skull

Much of the material in this chapter was found with the aid of the index to Ginzberg's *Legends of the Jews* under 'Foundation Stone' and 'Melchizedek', but I owe my reference to the Batu-Ribn of the Semang and to some places in Palestine to Eliade's *Myth of the Eternal Return*. An article by F. J. Hollis in *Myth and Ritual*, the first symposium edited by S. H. Hooke, considers the evidence for worship of the sun on the site of the Temple at Jerusalem. On the Akedah, the sacrifice of Isaac, I have learnt much from the second part of *The Springs of Creativity* by Heinz Westman. The archaeological evidence in regard to ritual infanticide is collected by W. F. Albright in *Yahweh and the Gods of Canaan*, pp. 203–11. This also was brought to my attention by Mr Westman, though he and I draw a different inference from it.

On the Melchizedekians the primary authorities are the *Philosophoumena of Hippolytus* (Book 7, ch. 8, c. 200 A.D.), the *Ecclesiastical History of Eusebius* (Book 5, ch. 28) written in the fourth century, and material collected by Epiphanius for his

Two depictions of Joachim and Anna from the
thirteenth-century window in the Lady Chapel
at Le Mans Cathedral.

Panarion, completed about 375, from much older authorities.
This is in the *Patrologia Graeco-Latina* (henceforth cited as
P.G.) in volume 41, columns 971–90. Other early materials are
in *The Book of the Cave of Treasures,* a Syriac text of the sixth
century translated and edited by Sir E. A. Wallis Budge for the
Religious Tract Society in 1927, with extracts from *The Book
of the Bee* (*c.* 1222) and from the Arabic *Annals* of Eutychius of
Alexandria, finished in 937. Some of this material may be
derived directly or indirectly from Julius Africanus (*c.* 240),
whose fragments were collected by Martin Routh in the
second volume of *Reliquiae Sacrae.* He certainly held that
Adam was buried at Golgotha. The form of the story of
Melchizedek in which he was born before the flood and after
the death of his mother Soponima, the sister-in-law of Noah,
is found in some manuscripts of *The Book of the Secrets of
Enoch,* and appended to the edition of this by R. H. Charles.

My knowledge of the sites in Jerusalem I owe to the expert
guidance of my brother, Canon Edward Every of St George's
Close there, and my introduction to the Samaritans and to
Mount Gerizim to him and Miss Ruth Black. In *The Legendary History of the Cross* I have generally followed a book of this
name by John Ashton, itself following a Dutch original of
1483. But much of the same material is in *The Golden Legend*
of Jacob de Voragine, of which Caxton's version is in The
Temple Classics.

The form of the story followed by Malory in chapters
5 and 6 of Book 17 in *The Morte d'Arthur* is based on

one that is common to two earlier versions of the quest for the Holy Grail, both written in French before 1225 and probably after 1210. Albert Pauphilet in his *Etudes sur la Queste del Saint Graal* (Paris 1921, pp. 144–55) thought it was the composition of the author of the *Queste* on the basis of the legend of the cross, but in his own edition of the *Queste del Saint Graal* (Paris 1923), he treated it as older than the *Queste* or the *Estoire,* sometimes called the *Grand Saint Graal.* I am sure that there is material in it that has not been properly assimilated to either, and that the Eve here is a mother-goddess figure, 'the mother of all living', rather than a feminine version of the Adam of the *Legend of the Cross.* In relating these tales to the real history of the holy places in Jerusalem I have been helped by articles in the *Dictionnaire d'archéologie chrétienne et de liturgie,* (henceforth *DACL*) on 'Croix, invention de la' and 'Helène'.

The harrowing of hell

In this chapter I begin to use *New Testament Apocrypha,* edited by W. Schneemelcher and in English by R. McL. Wilson on the basis of an earlier work in German by E. Hennecke. This supersedes *The Apocryphal New Testament* by M. R. James. Provision for the exorcism of candidates for baptism is made in *The Apostolic Tradition* of Hippolytus and elsewhere in *Documents of the Baptismal Liturgy,* edited by E. C. Whitaker for the Alcuin Club. Two early accounts of the materialisation of the Word of God in a human baby are found in *The Ascension of Isaiah* edited by R. H. Charles, where he simply appears on the floor of the home, and in a passage in *The Protevangelium of James* which I believe to be an interpolation. An interpretation of the paintings in the Roman catacombs in *The Baptism of Art* (1949) by the Russian scholar Wladimir Weidlé is still most useful. Articles in *DACL* are useful on particular subjects such as Orpheus. The use of allegory is dicussed from different points of view by Père Jean, now Cardinal Daniélou, in *Origen,* and by R. P. C. Hanson in *Allegory and Event.*

References to the discussion on deceit and ransom can be found in Hastings Rashdall's Bampton lectures of 1915 on *The Idea of Atonement in Christian Theology* (Macmillan 1920) and in the *History of the Doctrine of the Work of Christ* by R. S. Franks. The quotations from St Gregory of Nyssa come from chapter 22 of his *Great Catechetical Oration,* and those from the other St Gregory, of Nazianus, from *P.G.* 36, col. 653. St Augustine's definition of sacrifice is in chapter 6 of Book 10 of his *City of God.* St Anselm, who died in 1112, was the first person to write a whole book on the atonement as distinct from the incarnation, and he did not know that he was doing it; he called the book *Cur Deus homo,* 'Why God was made man'.

Lives of the Virgin Mary

Much of the material in this chapter comes from *New Testament Apocrypha,* edited by Schneemelcher and Wilson. In *Coptic Apocryphal Gospels* edited by Forbes Robinson I have used his translation of Anna singing to her baby in a Sahidic fragment on page 13, and of Bohairic accounts of the Virgin's death. The historical problem is the relation between the

The Journey of the Three Kings following the star to Bethlehem as represented in Cotton MS Nero c. iv, f. 12, of the twelfth century. British Museum.
Right:
A Virgin and child in marble from the Tyrol, of the twelfth or thirteenth century. Victoria and Albert Museum.
Overleaf:
Among the symbolic emblems around this ivory crucifixion the most interesting are at the foot of the cross. The earth is represented on the right as a mother with children and the ancient earthworm, the python. On the left is the sea and sea-monster is ridden by a human figure. Over both of these symbols of fertility religion rises the cross. A book cover made for the cathedral at Verdun in Lorraine in the early tenth century. Victoria and Albert Museum.

Syriac *History of the Blessed Virgin Mary*, published and translated by Sir E. A. Wallis Budge for Luzac's *Semitic text and translation* series and, on the one hand the *Protevangelium of James*, on the other the two or three Jewish-Christian gospels that survive only in fragments. The editor, M. Testuz, of the oldest manuscript of the *Protevangelium, Papyrus Bodmer V*, assigns it to the third century, but he and others allow that this already contains additions to the original. Budge's book is based on a copy made for him by an Assyrian (Nestorian) Christian of a Syriac manuscript written as late as the thirteenth or fourteenth century. This is evidently a composite collection of traditions, but here and there contains matter unlikely to have been invented by a later hagiographer. The most striking instance is the apparent identification of Mary the mother of James and Joses in the Gospels (*Mark* 15.27 and elsewhere) with the first wife of St Joseph.

The Byzantine commentator Theophylact of Bulgaria (*c.* 1100), writing of *St Matthew* 13.55 and *Galatians* 1.19 in *P.G.* 123, col. 293, maintained that Joseph's first wife was the widow of his brother Cleopas, and that he married her 'to raise up seed' under the conditions known as 'levirate marriage' (*Deuteronomy* 25.5–6, *St Mark* 12.18–25). By her he had four sons and two daughters, Salome and Mary of Cleopas (St John 19.25), so called because she was regarded as a daughter for Cleopas, not because she was his wife. Theophylact distinguished between this Mary and the Mary of James and Joses, whom he identified with Mary the mother of Jesus on the ground that she brought them up. The great scholar J. B. Lightfoot, who called attention to this in the later editions of his commentary on *Galatians*, regarded Theophylact's view as a compromise between St Jerome's insistence that 'the Lord's brothers' were children of Mary of Cleopas, and cousins of Jesus, and the view generally held in the east that they were sons of Joseph by a previous marriage. But on pp. 276–8 of the same commentary he collected quotations made by Eusebius from Hegesippus, a Jewish Christian writing in Palestine about 160, who distinguished between James and Jude, whom he regarded as sons of Joseph, and Simon or Simeon, the son of Cleopas and their cousin.

Simon seems to have succeeded James as Bishop of Jerusalem when he died in 62 or 66, and there is some evidence that he was alive as late as 107. As he comes last in the list of the family in *Mark* 6.3, it may be that Theophylact or his source rightly distinguished between his mother, Mary of Cleopas, and Mary of James and Joses, and that he was a grandchild brought up in the household. This could also account for the way in which other material in infancy gospels tends to be attributed to him.

The letter of Polycrates of Smyrna to Victor of Rome about St John wearing a priestly *petalon* or plate is quoted twice in the *Ecclesiastical History* of Eusebius (Book 3, ch. 31, Book 5, ch. 24). The sermon of St Gregory Palamas on the ancestors of the Virgin was translated from a rare Greek edition in *The Eastern Churches Quarterly* X, 8 (1954–5). The same number has a note by an Orthodox priest on Eastern Christian attitudes

to the immaculate conception of the Virgin. Some account of
the pagan biographical cycles which to some extent underlie
the iconography, and therefore the development of the story of
the Virgin's life and death, may be found in André Grabar's
Christian Iconography, a study of its origins, especially on pp.
80–82 and 102–4.

Lives of the Saints

The apocryphal acts and apocalypses are now most conveniently studied in *New Testament Apocrypha.* Fuller
translations of the *Clementine Homilies and Recognitions,* and a
volume of *Apocryphal Gospels, Acts and Revelations* are in the
Ante-Nicene Christian Library, recently reproduced in
America, but for the assessment of these in the light of later
discoveries we have to look to Schneemelcher and Wilson. On
the passions of the martyrs *Les Origines du culte des martyrs* by
Père Hippolyte Delahaye is still invaluable. The life of St
Cyril the Phileote, who died about 1110, has been edited with
a French translation and introduction by E. Sarcologos in the
Bollandist *Subsidia Hagiographica* 39. The best stories in the
Pratum Spirituale of John Moschus were collected by Norman
Baynes for an article in 1947, reprinted in his *Byzantine Studies
and other Essays.* An edition with a French translation in the
series *Sources Chrétiennes* is out of print. The peregrinations of
St Cuthbert's bones are recorded in the *Liber de miraculis
beati Cuthberti* of Reginald of Durham, who wrote in the
twelfth century, published by the Surtees Society in their
first collection. The story of Eilaff, the fox and the cheese I
found in *English Picnics* by Georgina Battiscombe. On the
thorny subject of the Holy Grail I have read, besides Miss
Weston's books, the most recent account of *The Evolution of
the Grail Legend* by D. D. R. Owen. No one else, so far as I
know, has connected the symbol with early Christian ways of
keeping the eucharistic elements at home, but very little was
known about these until the *Apostolic Tradition of Hippolytus*
was identified as his in 1916, and then those who were most
pleased with the evidence for the antiquity of reservation did
not always notice how it was done. So far as I can see the holy
bread, probably dipped in the cup, was taken home and placed
in another holy vessel. To this other wine was added and
consecrated by contact day by day. In times of persecution or
in the absence of a priest this could go on for a long time.
Something like this is likely to be the origin of the Grail
symbol, but this is not to deny its association with other
symbols of refreshment.

Some of the most thorough work on the sources of the life of
St Francis has been done by the Bishop of Ripon, Dr J. R. H.
Moorman, in a book on the sources published by Manchester
University in 1940, in his small but valuable *Life of St Francis*
and his collection of non-Franciscan stories about him, *The
New Fioretti.* The evidence for the antiquity of 'the breviary
of St Francis' was first produced by S. J. P. Van Dijk in
Franciscan Studies ix (1949) and summarised in *The Origins of
the Modern Roman Liturgy* by him and J. Hazelden Walker.
Dante's letter to Can Grande is translated in the Temple
Classics edition of his Latin works.

Visions of the afterlife

Translations of the Ethiopian version of the *Apocalypse of St Peter*, and of fragments and quotations from the Greek found elsewhere, are in the second volume of *New Testament Apocrypha. The Passion of St Perpetua and St Felicity* was edited with a new translation by Walter Shewring of this and of two sermons of St Augustine. St Augustine's views on the case of Dinocrates are in two places in his *De anima et eius orgine,* in Book 1, ch. 10, and Book 3, ch. 9. The repetition may serve to show how much he was worried by the problem of small children.

I owe my knowledge of the sermon *On the celestial powers* to the chapter on eschatology in *The Russian Religious Mind* by George Fedotoff, and the visions of Theodora to this and to L. Reau's *Iconographie de l'art chrétien* vol. ii, pp. 735–6. The Greek text is edited by Veselovsky in *Sbornik otdeleniya russkago yazika i slovesnosti* (St Petersburg 1890), where the visions occupy seventy pages. I have turned for my details to Liutprand's account of his embassy in *Scriptores rerum Germanicarum in usum scholarum* and to the *Book of the Eparch* or *the Prefect,* which was in force at the time. The stories from the *Dialogues* of Pope Gregory the Great are in Book IV, ch. 36–40. Those told by Bede are in his church history of England, of Fursa at Book III, ch. 9, and of Drythelm at Book V, c. 12. In the history of masses for the dead I have been helped by Chavasse's edition of *The Gelasian Sacramentary* as well as by articles in *DACL* on *défunts* and on *mort.* Raoul Glaber's story of the devils who knew all about Cluny is in *Patrologia Latina* 142, ch. 692, and the other version at ch. 926 in the same volume, in Jotsald's life of the Abbot Odilo. The life of St Brendan has been translated by J. F. Webb in a Penguin *Lives of the Saints* (1965). Evidence that the *Apocalypse of the Virgin* was known in some form in Ireland is in an article in the *Journal of Theological Studies* xxiii (1921), pp. 36–43, by St John D. Seymour on an Irish *Transitus Mariae* of the fourteenth century in which the respite is only for three hours on Sunday afternoons. A critical account of the stories connected with Lough Derg was given in *St Patrick's Purgatory* by Thomas Wright, who also edited *The Historical Works of Giraldus Cambrensis* (Gerald of Wales) for the Bohn library series of translations. A more sympathetic view was taken by S. Baring-Gould in *Curious Myths of the Middle Ages.*

The necessity of mythology

What Whitehead has to say about 'objective immortality' he said most fully in *Process and Reality.* The *Christian Topography* of Cosmas Indicopleustes is in *P.G.* 88. The controversy over Arthur Bury's *Naked Gospel,* an 'Honest to God' of the late seventeenth century, is described in my *High Church Party, 1688–1718,* pp. 75–7. An introduction to the German debate on Rudolf Bultmann's demythologising of the Gospels in existentialist terms may be found in *Kerygma and Myth,* of which the English translation, with one additional essay in English, was published in two volumes in 1953 and 1962. The Romanian theologian is Dumitriu Staniloae in an article in *The Eastern Churches Review,* II 4 (1969).

Further Reading List

Adamnan. *The Life of St Columba,* ed. T. Fowler, Oxford University Press, 1894. A translation by Wentworth Huyshe was later published by Routledge.

Apocrypha and Pseudepigrapha of the Old Testament. Translated and edited R. H. Charles, Oxford University Press 1963–65.

Ashton, John. *The Legendary History of the Cross.* Fisher Unwin, 1887.

Baring-Gould, S. *Curious Myths of the Middle Ages.* 2 vols. Rivington, 1868.
Lives of the Saints. 16 vols. Nimmo, 1897.

Dawes, E. and Baynes, N.H. *Three Byzantine Saints.* Blackwell, 1948.

Delahaye, Hippolyte. *Les Légendes Hagiographiques.* Bollandists, Brussels.
Origines du Culte des Martyrs. Bollandists, 2nd ed. 1906.

Dictionnaire d'Archéologie Chrétien et de Liturgie. Letourzey et Ane, Paris, 1907–52.

Eliade, Mircea. *Myth and Reality.* Harper, New York, 1963; Allen and Unwin, 1964.

Frankfort, H. and others. *Before Philosophy.* Penguin, 1949.

Ginzberg, Louis. *Legends of the Jews.* Jewish Publication Society, Philadelphia, 1925.

Gordon, Cyrus H. *Before the Bible.* Collins, 1962

Grunwald, Constantine de. *Saints of Russia.* Trans. Roger Capel, Hutchinson, 1960.

History of the Blessed Virgin Mary and History of the Likeness of Christ. Syriac texts with translations by E. A. Wallis Budge. Luzac, 1899.

Hutton, W. H. *English Saints.* Wells, Gardner and Darton, 1903.

Lang, David M. *Lives and Legends of the Georgian Saints.* Allen and Unwin, 1956.

Lévi-Strauss, Claude. *The Savage Mind.* English translation, Weidenfeld and Nicolson, 1960.

New Testament Apocrypha. Translated and edited by various authors. Lutterworth Press, 1963–65.

Prime W. C. *Holy Cross, a History of the Invention, Preservation and Disappearance of the Wood known as the True Cross.* Sampson Low.

Rice, Tamara Talbot. *Russian Icons.* Spring Books, Hamlyn, 1963.

Acknowledgments

The publishers acknowledge the following sources for permission to reproduce the illustrations indicated

COLOUR. Front cover: Musée Nicolas Sursock, Beyrouth. 6-7: Hirmer Verlag. 10: Pierpont Morgan Library. 14: Scala. 15: Roger Wood. 19: Bibliothèque Nationale. 23: National Gallery, London. 37: Eric Lessing – Magnum. 41: Meyer. 44: Denis Hughes-Gilbey. 45, 48: Giraudon. 61: Archivo Fotografico dei Civici Musei, Milan. 64: The Green Studio, Dublin. 68-9: Hann Collection. 72: John Massey Stewart. 85: Museo del Prado, Madrid. 88-9: J. C. W. Blatch. 92: Scala. 96: Ara Guler. 109: Giraudon. 112-3: Scala. 117: Giraudon. 120: Josephine Powell. Back cover: Hans Hinz.
BLACK & WHITE. Endpapers: Alinari. 8-9: Paul Popper. 12: Victoria & Albert Museum. 13, 16: British Museum. 17 left: Kungl Bibliteka, Stockholm. 17 right: Hirmer Verlag. 20: Alinari-Anderson. 21: Zodiaque. 24: Roger Viollet. 25 left: Archives Photographique, Paris. 25 right: Bulloz. 26 top: British Museum. 26 bottom: Giraudon. 27, 28, 29: Bodleian Library, Oxford. 30: Alinari. 31: Hamlyn Group Library. 32 left: Scala. 32-3: Alinari. 34-5: Giraudon. 36: Victoria & Albert Museum. 38-9: Stoedtner-Klemm, Dusseldorf. 42: British Museum. 43 bottom: Bodleian Library, Oxford. 46 left: Historisk Museum, Bergen. 46 right: British Museum. 47: Trinity College Library, Cambridge. 50 top: Ali Zaarour. 50 bottom: Alinari. 51 Giraudon. 52-3 top: Alinari. 52-3 bottom: V. & N. Tombazi, Athens. 53, 54-5: Alinari. 54: Irmgard Groth Kimball. 56-7: Bibliothèque Royale, Brussels. 58: David Hope. 59: Universitets Oldsaksamling, Oslo. 62: Alinari. 63: Archives Photographique, Paris. 66 left: Pont. Comm. di Arch. Sacra, Rome. 66-7: Alinari. 67: J. Lassus. 70: John Webb. 71 left: Alinari. 71 right: John Freeman. 74: Alinari. 75 top: Historisk Museum, Bergen. 75 bottom: Stoedtner-Klemm, Dusseldorf. 76-7: Alinari-Anderson. 78:9: Stoedtner-Klemm. 80: British Museum. 81 top: Jean Roubier. 81 bottom, 82: Archives Photographique, Paris. 83 right: A.C.L. Brussels. 84 top: British Museum. 84 bottom: Giraudon. 86: Hirmer Verlag. 86-7: Deutschen Arch. Inst 87: British Museum. 90-91: Anderson. 91: Deutschen Arch. Inst. 94: Anderson. 95 left: Mansell Collection. 95 right: Hamlyn Group Library. 97: National Gallery, London. 98-9: Roger Viollet. 100 left: Museo del Prado. 100 right, 101 left and bottom: Bibliothèque Nationale, Paris. 101 right: Staatliche Museen, Berlin. 102: Copyright reserved. 103: Alte Pinakothek, Munich. 104: Archivo Fotografico Vaticano. 105: Pierpont Morgan Library, New York. 106-7: Roger Viollet. 110: Yale Univ. Art Gallery. 111: Trinity College Library, Cambridge. 114-5: Victoria & Albert Museum. 115: Universitas Bibliotek, Heidelberg. 118: Rex Roberts Studios, Ltd. 119 top: Boudot-Lamotte. 119 bottom: Centro Elicotteri. 122,123: Alinari. 124: Archives Photographique, Paris. 125: Jean Roubier. 126-7: Bavaria Verlag. 128-9: Hirmer Verlag. 130-1: Held-Ziolo. 131: Bibliothèque Royale, Brussels. 132, 133: Archives Photographique, Paris. 134-5: British Museum. 135, 136-7: Victoria & Albert Museum.

Index